20 Powerful Women in Network Marketing
Tell All

20 Powerful Women in Network Marketing Tell All

Vol.1

Deborah Drummond & Caroline Blanchard

20 Powerful Women in Network Marketing Tell All – Vol. 1
Copyright © 2021 Deborah Drummond & Caroline Blanchard

Library and Archives Canada Publication Data is available upon request.
Print ISBN: 978-1-989146-13-2
eBook ISBN: 978-1-989146-14-9

Cover Design and Interior Design by A Beautiful Life Publishing

Printed in Canada

Contents

BOOK DEDICATION

To Audrey, Billie and Nicolas. You are my "WHY" for breathing, living, thriving and always wanting to better myself. You are my everyday inspiration, my everything, and I adore you.

Caroline xo

I'd like to dedicate this book to three women in particular that in my early years, impressed upon me to, no matter what, do what it takes to provide for your family.

That being my grandmother, my mother and my aunt. My grandmother Barbara Brown was a very strong woman who really didn't give warrant to what people thought of her, allowing her to step out of social expectations and be comfortable with herself. My aunt, Sandra Dickey was incredible at relationship building, and my mother, Lucky Harris, taught me my first experience of direct sales by taking me along to home party events and impressed upon me that there's always a way to take care of family.

I would also like to dedicate this first book that I am a part of to all the women that have made an impression upon me through the years to be brave. I would pull strength from women I didn't know personally but was empowered by their courage. Women like Gloria Steinem, Patricia Ireland and many others. Women entrepreneurs were not always accepted when I first started in owning my own businesses. In my early years, having female coaches like Kim Evans, Carolyn Cooper Mc Outt, and Daphne Mc Keen made me feel supported. I thank them for their alliance with me, being my sisters in life and in business.

I would also like to dedicate to Caroline Blanchard, my co-publisher, in this venture and the many we do together on her incredible stealth of wisdom and ability to shine a light on the best parts of me when I can't see them. My dearest friends, in time and years – Debbie Hawes and Pete Holt (aka Limmy), and Lyza Ulrich who are simply my pillars in life, they remind me of how far I have come as we have walked this path called life together it reminds me to be grateful for what I have and to not be scared to show who I am and where I have come from.

Absolutely, all that I do and all that I am fills my heart like no other feeling than to be the mother to my incredible daughter Chloae, whose articulation of life and her level of intelligence of people leaves me in awe... and her love for books, her whole life was such an incredible thing to watch as she was growing up and to be granted the grace to be part of a book with a plethora of incredibly powerful women and to be able to dedicate that to her is an incredible feeling and to my incredibly talented, creative-minded son, Ocean who impresses me often with his love for music and eye for fashion. He reminds me every day to stay cool, stay calm and just let things unfold.

Thank you for reading our book. I hope that in this book, you find your way to becoming "gentle to yourself but powerful to the world" type of woman in business that brings you satisfaction and joy.

Deborah Drummond

PREFACE

Thank you for reading this book, which is a powerful collection of words and stories. In these real-life experiences, you'll discover, feel and learn the power of entrepreneurship in action.

The hope for us is that, whether you have never been in network marketing before or are a legend in this industry, you find a "piece of gemstone advice" in this book and feel reassured or inspired to take action in ways that bring you success.

We believe in this industry to the depths of our hearts and know this industry has changed, empowered, rescued and elevated millions of women already.

We are extremely grateful to the women pioneers of this industry who have walked before us, creating paths for us to follow. We are equally grateful for women, like the authors of this book, who continue forging ahead and laying track for it to be easier for women of all ages and backgrounds to enter this incredible industry and surpass any dreams they could possibly imagine.

It has been an honour for us to align with these powerful women to produce this book, and we hope you enjoy reading it as much as we did producing it.

In good health and happiness,

Deborah Drummond & Caroline Blanchard
The TRUE THAT Show Co-Hosts & Producers
TRUE THAT Media Publishers

1

DEBORAH DRUMMOND

I'm eight years old at the front door and I'm excited. Watching my mom pack her products that we're going to set up in my aunt's living room. I get to go work with my mom. She was a home party representative. I loved the feeling of hanging out with the ladies. I felt grown-up, and I enjoyed watching the women having fun, shopping, and laughing.

That was my first introduction to direct sales; it created great memories in my late teens. My mother got involved in a clothing company, and you know what? I had the same happy experience, my girlfriend's getting together, laughing, having fun and my mother having success. So, I have to say, that's probably part of the reason that when I got the vision to start my own home party company, I went for it.

Now to paint the scenario, I was a single mom of a beautiful young daughter, starting my own business for the first time. This was over 25 years ago; women entrepreneurs were not common.

Nor was the decision to launch two companies at once, both in health and wellness. Aromatherapy and gemstone jewelry were still unknown.

The story of how I created two home party companies for 17 years is an incredible journey meant to be its own book one day. My love for direct sales when I went into those companies was the same as when I came out, even if I didn't see myself going back to network marketing in the future. Throughout this whole time, I was a happy traditional business owner for 27 years.

When I got invited back into network marketing, it was because I was willing to help a fellow entrepreneur. When she asked me to look at the business, I nicely said no. She didn't know everything that was going on in my life. I was going through a marital status change, becoming a single mom of two children, had 18 staff, my business was open seven days a week, and we were booked 12 hours a day, three weeks ahead.

When she was telling me the company story, my head was saying no, but my gut was screaming yes. I said I was too busy, and she said, "I will back you all the way." Those were powerful words for me. Her words felt like relief. She was smart enough to give me a sample. I came home, gave it to my daughter, and she had amazing results; we both joined the company, and the rest is history.

I wasn't lying when I said I had no time. I sacrificed little things, I had to really structure the power of my moments, and I'd text every moment I had free. That's why I love network marketing, it's a group effort – in times where I was up against the clock. I could call people to help, and that's very different from traditional business.

I've chosen this as a career, I've chosen the products and the company that I'm with because it has allowed me to offer an extension of what I believe, which is preventative health and entrepreneurial wealth. Being the traditional business owner that I was, I always thought about legacy. I knew I was creating this business for myself, but I also was creating it for my family's financial future. Being a single mom, I knew that sometimes it's all on you, and you need to find the courage to go all in.

There have been wins and accomplishments I have been able to experience in my networking business—most of them, a complete surprise. I didn't expect the awards and perks, international travel, recognition from my peers, lifelong friendships and a plethora of incredible industry people that are living a fulfilled life.

Above all of the perks I have received, being able to spend time in this industry, working and building with my daughter was incredible. As a result of being raised in an entrepreneurial-minded home, watching my son deciding to be an entrepreneur at 17 and starting his own company makes me grateful to this industry.

People have told me that they see me as driven, but I would correct it by saying that I'm PURPOSE driven. When I really believe in something, I'm an "all in" woman. Life's not been easy every day just because I made an incredible lifestyle business decision, but with my willingness to learn, my commitment, excitement and desire for a better life for myself and for others, that has been the elixir I've woken up to every morning.

For some people, it's their coffee. For me, it's my fuel.

I was willing to stay up late, willing to get up early, willing to spend money on books, courses and was willing to go to company conference because they told me it was the best place to move my business quicker. One could even argue that I take as many courses, read more books, hire different coaches as much now as I did in the beginning of my business.

It wasn't funny then, but it's funny now when people tell me, "you deliver presentations so well", but they just don't remember seeing me at the very beginning of my career where I barely got thru a presentation without being so full of nerves I thought I would not make it to the end, it was all I could do to just stand there and say what I knew.

To answer one of the three "Tell All's" that created my success, the word that comes to me is GRACE. That may not sound like much advice, but it really is. Business isn't always easy. There's time we feel confused, we feel we're not getting traction, we get frustrated, and it feels hard. I feel Grace has got me out of those places and back into hope and joy.

Grace for me gets banked up every time I work my business, do training, have a success, help someone hit a goal, stretch myself, take a risk, so when I feel like I'm hitting the wall, all that activity banks up Grace for me and makes tough times easier.

Another one of my "Tell All's" is definitely HIRING COACHES AND PROFESSIONALS that know more than I do, in an area I want to get better at.

My next tell-all is, and this might sound a little, what some would say, "Janis Joplin", but sometimes YOU JUST GOT TO SUCK IT UP AND JUMP. Sometimes you just got to go all in, no matter whether you know how it'll work out, sometimes push comes to shove, and I have had to shove myself. I have to take that risk. I have to call that person that I am nervous about, I have to ask for a sale that I might be unsure of and I have to bypass my own self-defeating talk and tell myself "no more excuses, no more avoiding, just do it!"

Here is one more "Tell All" that is one of my success secrets on days that I'm not 100 percent feeling "it," I use MUSIC. I find a song that's going to put me in a different headspace, and I listen to it really loud. If I need to feel brave, I listen to AC/DC. If I need to get calm and centred, I listen to some Chris Stapleton. If I need inspiration, I listen to Peter Gabriel. If I want to be kind to myself, I listen to Loretta Lynn. If I want to feel safe, I listen to Fleetwood Mac. Everyone has their own way of overcoming feelings and thoughts that hold them back. For me, I have found a solution in music. It may sound a little odd or unorthodox, but music has truly made a difference in my business success.

Here is another one of my powerful success tools I will share: WRITE. If you were to look at my desk right now, you would see writing on whiteboards, pads of paper, journals and daytimers. I have been called Paper Girl more than once. I use a daytimer that lines out for me questions that I ask myself in the morning that prompts me to think intentionally about how that day is going to go. I plan the night before my day ahead. I also have a writing system for evaluating my day and how to close my evening out.

MAKE LISTS. Whether it's a grocery list, personal development list, prospect list, Christmas list, goals list, financial goals list, time-lining or self-evaluation, making lists has also been a critical part of my business results.

Lastly, I am an avid reader. READING is crucial to achieving success, in my opinion. As I sit in my home right now on one chair, there's three books, there's one book to the left to me, three more books to the right of me and four on my bedside table. I love to read actual books with paper. I love to underline, circle, make a star, and I really like to dog-ear the pages.

For me, this thing called life, of which my career is a part of has been such an untold series of events that I couldn't have put together on my own. I have had to learn to have faith, have patience, have trust; trust in myself has been one of the biggest lessons in my life. What I do to make this journey better, easier, faster, less painful and more joyful is to do my best to stay aligned with myself and the right people.

I think that this is an incredible industry. I love the magic in it. I love the hope in it. I've seen people accomplish goals in half the time or double the time, and it can be as frustrating as it is exhilarating. I absolutely love how at the heart of this industry it is about helping others. All we can do is be who we are in what we do.

I have to say sometimes our industry gets a bad rap because people didn't get what they wanted either fast enough, smooth enough or easy enough, or, or, or... There are so many pieces to success in this industry, not unlike traditional business. People leave for whatever reason, and that's okay. I just never want to see anyone leave before that tipping point where traction hits the road and it starts to reveal the dreams they have for themselves.

I'm really happy and honoured to be an author in a book whose mandate is to raise the bar on the how people see the professionalism of this incredible industry. I truly believe that it is an industry for everybody. I've said it before and I will always say it that in my opinion network marketing is the most equal opportunity employer I have yet to see in my lifetime.

Thank you for the opportunity to share. I hope you found something in my story that inspired you, helped you, or even made you laugh.

If you could go back in time when you started your first business in network marketing and you could start all over again, what would you do differently?

I would tell myself to get comfortable being uncomfortable. I would tell myself that it's when I'm uncomfortable that I'm growing myself and my check.

Be patient. I think that I can get so excited about what I want and need that having it happen quickly becomes a strong desire—being impatient with not getting to the levels that I wanted in my business as fast as I wanted created unnecessary uncertainty.

I would also tell myself and affirm to myself more often that I am enough, I know enough, my skills are enough to get me to wherever it is that I want to go.

I would also remind myself that faith is going to be a major component of my happiness.

———

Deborah loves her country, Canada, and loves the world. Her two favourite people in the universe are her incredible daughter, Chloae, and her amazing son, Ocean.

Deborah owned a private health practice and has personally worked on over 30,000 clients. She has formulated hundreds of natural formulas and is a pioneer of taking holistic products to market.

She says at the beginning of her career, she was sometimes called a hippie, and now she is known as a successful professional hippie.

Deborah has been an entrepreneur since her 20s and is a well-known keynote speaker and recognized internationally for her accolades as a woman in business.

She dedicates an incredible amount of time speaking, teaching and mentoring and is highly recognized in radio, TV and print and is the Co-Founder of The TRUE THAT Show.

2

CAROLINE BLANCHARD

Network marketing is truly the greatest equalizer of all industries. People from any age, background, education level, style, gender or ethnicity can be successful at it as long as they have the DESIRE to make it happen!

We all have our reasons and motivating factors to join this industry. For me, what drives me is securing my future and my children's future, and helping women be successful, confident, find and live their purpose, and feel worthy as their own person. Quite often, as women, or caretakers, or moms, we lose our personal identity, and we don't know our self-worth anymore. Network marketing allows us to build something that is ours and makes us feel empowered.

Network marketing was a major contributor to changing and improving my life. It played a large role in motivating me to find my own identity through a lot of work and self-development and be okay with who I am. I went from being a very insecure woman inside who hated her body, appearance and self in general to striving to be better and learning to love and appreciate myself because I AM enough.

I have to admit that most of my life, I felt like an imposter because the perception people had of me was so different than the one I had of myself! I carried the feeling that I didn't belong, was unworthy and "defective." People would tell me how smart, talented, fun and beautiful I was, and every time I was thinking to myself: "Are you kidding me? You clearly don't know me. If you'd really know me, you'd change your mind and leave." So I've always been careful not to get too attached or involved with anyone.

I feel it's important to share with you a little insight on me, one of the words that can describe me really well is "survivor." I'd never identified with that word until recently because I went through life, leaving the bad experiences in the past, dissociating from them and numbing the rest that was lingering. I did survive quite a few traumas though, from growing up with no father, to being abused the first time at the age of 5, to being bullied and beaten up, with a lot in between. But for some reason I can't explain, I always kept my chin up, and I think that's what saved me. A part of me was suffering and drowning in depression since I was little, but I always refused to make it my reality. I chose, subconsciously, at a very young age to put on a mask of a happy, caring and strong person and "just get through it." I've always been passionate about fighting for justice, equality, rescuing animals and anyone who needed rescue. I now feel that I did, and do that because for so many years, being saved and accepted is what I needed most.

I've never had self-esteem or self-confidence, but I got so good at faking it that I always had the reputation and image of being strong and self-confident, and it always helped me succeed and be an over-achiever in all my jobs, projects and ventures.

My life was not the definition of what easy or simple is, but I wouldn't change it for the world as it made me the person I am today with what I have today. I've learned resilience at a young age, to not dwell on what hurts and always look in front of me. It was the only thing I could do. Whatever situation I've been in, I always tried to seek the good in it. A part of me has always been grateful, and I always chose to look at the brighter side of things.

I did feel like quitting life a few times, and even try it at some point, until I was 24 and became a mother. At that point, I finally understood my reason for living and what I had been waiting for all along. Life really started for me the day I looked into my son's eyes. I knew everything would be okay and felt what I had never felt before; pure, unconditional, endless love and some peace and happiness. I NOW had a reason to live. In the following years, I had two gorgeous daughters, and I love them just as much! My children are the biggest blessing I ever had, and they are my WHY. Why I do everything I do. Why I stuck it through. Why I joined this business and committed to building a legacy.

I feel it is by pure serendipity that I left the big corporate world at the age of 37 and join the Network Marketing industry. Sometimes our prayers are answered in ways we would never expect. I wanted the internal pain to go away, and I wanted something to change in my life, but I didn't know it would come this way!

I've been numbing my pain since I was 12 with alcohol, drugs and medication without anyone ever knowing I was doing it or going through pain. I've always been an over-achiever and a highly functional mom/career woman/volunteer and always had a very happy, fun and strong "front." Until one day, burned-out from my very high-stress, demanding position and dealing with the recent passing of my father, I clearly lost any sense of judgement and logic and had a few drinks and pills. I later woke up in ICU, lucky to still be alive. Everyone thought I wanted to die, but I didn't. I adored my kids way too much for that. I just wanted to stop "feeling" for a moment, and it got totally out of hand.

That event was the answer to my prayers and changed the course of my life for the best. I had to admit to myself and the world I had a drinking problem and an addiction to sleeping pills. No one thought so because I was just taking a few glasses of wine every day, and the doctor was prescribing me those pills; not a big deal, right? Except it WAS a big deal! I had been drinking since I was 12 to numb the pain and anxiety. I was never drunk and was highly functional, productive, involved in my community, fun, successful and responsible; I had never missed a day of work, a kid's event or a deadline! I was rocking it… on the outside! But the outside wasn't matching the inside, and it was now time to merge them, and I needed help.

Three months after that day, I quit my high-paid position because I knew in my heart it wasn't aligned with my personal values anymore and started a daily external rehab program for 6 weeks. For 6 weeks, I went to face my demons every day, from 9 am to 3 pm while my kids were in school. In that period, I faced myself, not the businesswoman and over-achiever, but the mother, the hurt child in me and the alcoholic and addict, which were the hardest titles ever to accept. By completing the six weeks, I knew I could face this new sober life and changes ahead and felt lighter and stronger than ever.

Very shortly after, my friend heard about a network marketing company and got all excited about it and started throwing all the information at me. She told me I could put all of my own efforts to build my own paycheque, do it for my family and me and not for someone else. I'd be able to work around my kid's schedule and be able to STAY HOME WITH THEM. I'd have flexibility AND residual income at the same time. I'd no longer have a boss and pressure to produce. I could have all that without having to invest a huge amount of money. Most of all, we could do it together and help and support each other! The more I was listening to her, the more I felt a new energy living in me. She kept telling me that I would do so well, all of my strengths, qualities and etc. She really believed in me! She convinced me that I was worth it. She convinced me that I could actually do this thing. She believed in me way more than I believed in myself at the time. So I decided to jump in with her. I gave myself the biggest gift; I gave myself the permission to dream again!

I came home and told my husband I had just signed up with this company, and I was over-the-moon excited, and I would change the world and... bam! He busted my bubble in less than two minutes. He told me how I wasted money, it was a scam, people don't make money in this business, and I made a mistake and should get a real job instead, etc. I was very sad to not feel supported, but something in me was telling me I had to do it, and I did. It wasn't the greatest decision for us as a couple, but I chose me that day.

I dove in with not much training and made all the mistakes you can make and had so much negative self-talk, but somehow, never gave up. At some point towards the end of my time in this company, someone suggested that I read *The Slight Edge*, by Jeff Olson. This book brought a significant switch in my life. It changed my life philosophy. It instilled a discipline in me and made me realize I could do ANYTHING I wanted; I just had to see it, plan it, and work at it every single day.

It's really at that point that I also realized the company I was with wasn't aligned with my real values, but I knew the industry was where I belonged. So I visualized the ideal company I wanted, and shortly after, it appeared on my path. I was scared to make a change and start over, but I knew it was necessary and did.

This new company was perfectly aligned with my personal values, and I loved the culture and corporate leadership. This company also had a system in place that, at first, I refused to follow because I thought with all the sales experience I had and my Bachelor's and experience in Marketing, I could find ingenious ways to move my business faster. So for the first two years, I did it my way. I had some success but also plateaued very fast because I had a hard time duplicating myself.

After going to a few conferences and events, I kept seeing those people who were recognized on stage for being the biggest achievers or top earners, and they would always come back to the basics and the system I wasn't following. I finally admitted to myself that my way would not bring me where these people were. I decided to put aside everything I thought I knew and my ego, and started from scratch and followed the system. My business then shifted and started growing.

The people and leaders I needed on my road started showing up. I started attracting success because I was finally doing what was suggested with a system that had a track-proven record of success. My ascension was far from being a straight upward line, and there are many days I wanted to quit, but I had surrounded myself with people, like Deborah Drummond, who really believed in me, mentored me and never gave up on me. I started to eliminate my negative self-talk and believe I was worth having success and abundance. I still had failures and disappointments from time to time, but I learned to accept them as lessons and grow from it.

PREPARE to fail in this business and EMBRACE your failures. It WILL happen. A lot of people will tell you can't do it or will just plainly ignore you or your business. It's okay. Keep at it and follow your dream. Keep your desire, excitement and passion alive. Write your WHY and look at it every day. Stay focused and you will achieve what you set your mind to.

My 3 biggest "Tell All's" I will give you are the ones I feel helped me the most.

1. SELF- DEVELOPMENT

If you want to grow your business, you will have to grow yourself. Your business will never be bigger than you are. You absolutely need to make self-development a priority in your life.

Be disciplined. Every day, read ten pages of a good self-development book and listen to 15 minutes of a positive and constructive podcast. You need to fill your mind with positive words and knowledge that will help you grow and expand your horizons and mindset.

Write ten affirmations a day in the PRESENT tense, whether they be the same or different ones from the previous day, write them down!

List your dreams and create a vision board and look at it every single day.

The biggest challenge in your life and your biggest enemy will always be the tape playing in your mind until you press stop, eject it and insert a new one. Only you have the power to do this. You can make the decision in an instant, but it then becomes a daily practice to maintain that new positive story.

2. DAILY DISCIPLINES & CONSISTENCY – at least five days/ week

Do two new exposures a day. Expose your product or business by giving information, handing out a tool, sampling a product, showing a presentation or a video two times each day.

Do four follow-ups a day. I won't expand on this too much because there are books and webinars that will teach you how to follow-up successfully, but the secret to success is FOLLOW-UPS.

Before you go to bed at night, plan your tomorrow. Planning reduces stress and anxiety and increases productivity by so much.

Make it a habit to keep track of your activities and results at the end of each day, week and month. How many exposures and follow-up you did; your weekly and monthly pay cheque, how many new clients you had, how many people joined your team, your volume. Do it from day one in your business, even if it is zero. Write it down. In time, when you look back, you will see progress.

Progress is my biggest motivator, and it confirms I am going in the right direction. If you do your daily activities consistently, you will see progress for sure! You will also be able to clearly link your progress and success to your activity and be able to adjust and re-adjust.

Taking charge and responsibility for your life starts with your daily planning and activities. The day you truly accept you are responsible for everything in your life, you will start gaining control of your life and be able to succeed.

3. AUTHENTICITY

Always share from the heart. When you share your business and product, don't think about what it will do for you or how much commission it will pay. Always think about what it will do for the person in front of you. Offer solutions to that person and don't deliver a sales pitch.

Don't be attached to the outcome of your conversations and interactions; you don't have control over that. Be attached to what you CAN control; your activity and the quality and authenticity of your interactions.

In a nutshell, always know that you have choices. Learn to dream again and choose to live your dreams. Work your business like a business. Do it daily with authenticity, integrity and compassion. Believe in all the possibilities that lay ahead of you. Control your self-talk and always work on your mindset. You owe it to yourself. And don't quit. Ever. The only way to fail in this business is to quit. Everything else is a learning curve. Focus on the process and progress and not on the results. Find your mentors, be coachable and never give up! Happiness and success are a journey, not a destination.

If you could go back in time when you started your first business in network marketing and you could start all over again, what would you do differently?

I would not allow people whose contribution to my life is negative to take up as much space as they did. I would also commit sooner to being coachable and would put self-development as a priority from day one.

Caroline is a mother of 3 children she considers her life teachers. She also rescues animals, which adds up to having four dogs and one cat!

Having worked in the corporate world for over 20 years, she decided to leave it all to pursue her passion. She now helps people live, look, feel better, and run their own businesses.

3

CAROLYN AUGER

"Healing the wounds of my inner child has made me feel that I can accomplish absolutely anything that I put my mind to."

Truth be told, I have always been an entrepreneur and a networker. If I love a product or service, I will happily recommend it to others. I always knew that I needed to work for myself. I began my professional journey in 1988, graduating from McGill University with a Bachelor of Education in Physical Education & Fitness. Even then, I knew that I did not want to be confined to a classroom or have a stringent schedule, so I worked as a personal trainer for many years. I wanted the freedom to live my life on my own terms, and to me, that is the biggest asset of entrepreneurship.

I was blessed to be a stay at home mom and recognized the value in being there for my daughters, especially because of my own trauma filled childhood. As a child, I hated the end of a school day, and I wanted that to be different for my daughters. In 2006, when my daughters were both in high school, I went back to school for my certification in massotherapy. Once again, I knew that I could manage my own schedule and fulfill my desire to help others. Most importantly, I could still be there for my daughters; I could take vacations to match their school schedule and stay home with them when they were sick. The challenge with a career like this was that if I wasn't working, I wasn't making money.

In 2009, my godmother, who was my saviour in childhood, passed away. I spent three weeks sleeping at the hospital with her and was absolutely devastated when she was gone. This loss made me incapable of working for months. Massaging clients takes a lot of physical and emotional energy, energy I did not have after such a significant loss. I then recognized my need for a plan B, something to fall back on in case I had to end my career as a massage therapist. In life, being prepared is an important asset.

In 2012, an old friend from high school reached out to me about an online business in health and wellness. At first, I politely declined, not realizing that this was the opportunity I had been looking for all of this time. I had been approached by people working with different companies, but none of them had ever resonated with me. Although this company resonated with me, I was extremely skeptical of this new offer. I didn't see myself as a saleswoman nor as a party host, and I made it very clear that I would never present in front of a group of people. I am an introvert, quite shy by nature, although people often laugh at this remark. I guess I have done a good job at overcoming these fears while growing into a true entrepreneur. I have learned that a network marketing business is about much more than products or services being offered; it's just as much about personal development, self-discovery, self-determination and self-actualization.

As I looked into the company presented to me, there was something very intriguing. Something within me told me to take the leap of faith. Even though I didn't need my husband's permission, I did ask for his advice. He has always believed in me, supporting whatever decision I made. Sadly, over the years, I have seen so many spouses crush the dreams of their partners. I am very grateful for the continued support my husband always offered. Once I decided to join my friend's team, I was all in, and I wanted to tell absolutely everyone. I was so excited that I was unable to talk about anything other than my new business. My excitement did pay off, and I quickly had three brand new business partners on my team. The momentum was palpable, and my business was growing so fast. I became overwhelmed with excitement and obsessed with getting to the next level, acquiring a new title. Needless to say, I made too many mistakes, and my initial success (in title) was short-lived. I actually lost my title twice, which was a huge struggle. The loss was not what troubled me; it was the feeling that I was a fraud. While I was building my team again, I believed that I couldn't tell anyone that my business had fallen apart. That was challenging because I have always prided myself on being open and honest. I eventually recognized that the resilience it took to continue to work hard even after setbacks was something to celebrate and could help inspire and encourage others.

Network marketing is simply a different form of distribution. Many people find great success in the industry, yet many others hold misconceptions about it. This leads me to another huge obstacle that I had to overcome; the fear of being misperceived by others. Through personal development and self-actualization, I learned that I do not have control over the perceptions others may have of me. I was someone who had been very misunderstood for many years, and I had to learn to let go of those imposed perceptions. Some people look at my life and may see me as the woman with two 'failed' marriages. I am proud that I had the courage to leave not once but twice, as now I get to reap the benefits of a joyful and fulfilled marriage. What is most important is how I see myself, not how others see me. A huge lesson for me has been to disregard the negative comments directed towards me or the industry. Everyone has the right to their opinions; however, I have the power to not let these voices affect how I see myself and my business.

What is success to you? I know that I am extremely successful both professionally and personally, although the success didn't come easy. All the great things in life are worth the risk and hard work. I truly believe that any success comes from self-determination and having the courage to work at the challenges that may seem insurmountable. It's okay to figure things out as we go. We will never start our journeys knowing all of the answers from the onset. My greatest marker of success is the person I have become along the journey. I have worked very hard to overcome my childhood traumas. I strongly believe that healing the wounds of my inner child has made me feel that I can accomplish absolutely anything that I put my mind to. I have also discovered that a key to professional success is being content and at peace in your personal life.

If I could go back in time when I first started my business and could start all over again, what would I do differently?

To be honest, I am a true believer that things are meant to be exactly as they are. We are all meant to learn through experiences. That's how we grow and evolve, although there are many areas of my life where I would react differently or make better decisions. However, those mistakes are what have made me who I am today, and that is the whole point of life.

Having said that, with the wisdom and experience from the past eight and a half years, I would definitely have followed my own instincts more. Starting the business was so exciting, and it is so important to have that level of excitement. However, I would refrain from calling people and rambling on about how this business will change my life and theirs. Although it has been life-changing, nothing is immediate, and the message can sound unrealistic.

While it is great to have big dreams and goals, in my opinion, it is important to set goals that are realistic and make sense for the amount of time and energy you are ready to put into your business. There is a small percentage of people who make it to the top quickly. However, for most, this business takes time to grow. I definitely would have been more patient and learned how to properly coach new consultants. Each person has a unique set of skills, experiences and will have very different goals. I often made the mistake of putting too much pressure when new consultants were starting their business. I was making it about my goals. It's never about us, but about them.

If I were starting over today, I would also make better financial decisions. Starting a business in most industries usually requires a loan. In network marketing, it should be no different. I would budget my expenses for products, conferences, and resources to help me thrive and develop a plan to pay back the money I invested. Investing in the purchase of your products, kits, or tools is key, and it is the best way to learn about the product you will be recommending. People do this all this time for school or other businesses, so why is network marketing any different?

Although network marketing is a turnkey operation with all the website and marketing tools, you need many skills to be successful.

When I started my business, most communication occurred via email. Now everything is done via Facebook. That was a difficult transition for me. Social media still remains a bit of a struggle, but I have realized that it is a useful tool, although not the only tool. If you are starting your business and not savvy when it comes to social media, I would highly recommend asking or hiring someone to help you.

Personal development is key. I have always been working on myself to overcome the past, however, reading for personal growth is extremely important for the business. I highly recommend reading the pertinent books to learn more about the industry of network marketing. It is also important to read for personal growth, something I wish I had done sooner. Within personal development, we get to understand ourselves better. Scheduling specific hours for your business and having clear and simple objectives are both keys to your success. You may be working full time and will need to fit in a call before work or on your lunch hour. I didn't have a clear schedule for years. It makes it more difficult and made me feel as though I was always working my business when, in fact, I wasn't. I was just thinking about it.

I would have hired a coach outside the industry. You may want to consider that to help support you and ensure you have a clear plan of action. This will also help you when working with other people. Everyone starts their business for different reasons. Learn to be a good listener, and allow others to go at their own pace. Most people start their business alongside a full-time job, so guiding them to plan time in their schedule is crucial.

Be true to yourself, be authentic, and if you have good instincts, follow them. They will always guide you. Always keep in mind that, in actual fact, you are the product. People will be joining your business and purchasing products because they like and trust you. This is why building relationships and getting to know people is key.

Carolyn Auger is a self-published author of *With All My Heart* under the pseudonym, Elizabeth McLennan. One of Carolyn's goals is to inspire others to find their path towards healing their inner child. She continues to be fulfilled by helping others through her network marketing business, massage therapy practice, as well as, health and wellness coaching. Carolyn, and her husband, Steve, love working out, eating healthy, and they have fun creating videos to help inspire others to live healthier lifestyles.

4

MARILEE MARICICH

People may see me speaking in front of an audience of several thousand or know that I have a large network marketing business today, but they don't know what it took for me to get there. We all seem to have the tendency to look at someone who has had success and compare ourselves to them.

When we compare ourselves with someone who is further down the road on their journey, we are not being fair to ourselves. We don't know the struggles, setbacks, determination, and triumphs that it took for them to reach their goals and realize their success. Everyone has a story so let me tell you mine.

As a little girl, I knew down deep inside that I would one day do something of great significance. Yet, it was hard to imagine how that would ever be possible because I struggled with extreme shyness and anxiety. By the age of five, I was having full-blown Panic Attacks that followed me for many years.

After graduation, it seemed like all of my friends were venturing out from our hometown to chase their dreams. I also had a burning desire to make my mark on the world but secretly felt like a prisoner in my own skin... trapped in constant anxiety. "Playing it safe" became a survival skill and a way of life for me. Yet, the sense that I would do something of significance never stopped. I knew my life was meant for greater things.

With only a partial college education, but a fulltime creative thread running through me, I started working in Marketing & Interior Design, implementing my talents in the boating industry and the family-owned business I grew up in. I loved working alongside my dad, who is, to this day, one of the most entrepreneurial people I know. He taught me so much about dreaming big.

At the age of 22, I married my hometown sweetheart, Shawn. He worked extremely hard as a Commercial Fisherman in the Bering Sea of Alaska (If you have ever seen the television series "Deadliest Catch," you have a visual of what he did. Thankfully at the time, I did not). His schedule required him to be gone for several months at a time. It was high risk for high pay, but we were committed to being responsible with our money, with the goal of early retirement.

Then one day, I got a call from Alaska. Shawn was injured, and they were flying him back home, with what became a career-ending back injury. That once very secure paycheck was turned off. Our world, as we knew it, changed overnight. He spent over a year trying to rehabilitate his back so that he could return to work. My income just helped to pay the bills. His injury had changed the trajectory of our once comfortable financial game plan.

We realized what can happen when your primary source of income is dependent on your body, being able to perform a task. We knew we did not want to work for someone else and needed to recreate ourselves if we were really going to get ahead. So, we ventured out to pursue the "American Dream" and start our own business.

Recreating ourselves, we started a company specializing in high-end Yacht Detailing. Our client list grew quickly, and we found ourselves each working over 100 hours a week, in what seemed like an endless schedule. I am sure to everyone around us, it looked like life was great... and who would dare complain about having a successful business? But the truth was, I had no idea how to get off this hamster wheel. I never told a soul but was praying for something to change. We were back in the same situation that we started with... our paycheck was dependent on us showing up every day. If we took a day off, the paychecks stopped. If we were sick or injured and could not work, the paychecks stopped. There had to be a better way!

It was at that busiest time of my life that a neighbour reached out and wanted to show me a product that she had found. I barely had time to spend with family, let alone time to listen to a sales pitch. Yet, she kept following up with me and was convinced that I would love what she had to share. We joke about it now, but the only reason I agreed to finally meet with her was to get her off my back.

She came to my house to share her presentation, and even though she was as kind as could be, I had a total poker face as I listened. I did not show her the absolute shock I felt when she shared the income disclosure statement of how much people were making per month by creating a team of distributors and building a leveraged income. She talked about the trips you could earn and the fun that they were having working as a team while helping others feel and do better. It sparked something inside of me. Could this be an answer to my prayers?

Can you believe I told her that I was a hard NO for the business and was only interested in being a customer? The truth is that my fear and insecurities took over, and I told her that there was no way I could fit anything else into my already exhausting schedule. After she left, I could not stop thinking about something she asked earlier, "If you keep doing what you're doing, where will you be in 5 years?" I kept asking myself, "What If?" Then a few weeks later, I had a defining moment... I learned that she was still busy building her dream team and had started talking to MY friends about her products and the business opportunity behind it. My highly competitive spirit came alive, and I magically found the time to fit the business in my life, so I called her and said, "I'm IN"! I'm grateful to this day that she shared this industry with me.

I did not realize it at the time, but saying "Yes" to network marketing, would prove to be one of the most significant decisions of my life. I knew in my heart, from the very beginning, that God would use this to not only help me impact the lives of others in a positive way, but He would use this to change my life in a major way, for the better. This would prove to be the journey that would help me overcome my anxieties and the things that held me back from achieving my true potential.

I'll never forget my very first presentation. I was standing in the living room, in front of my very first audience. My heart was pounding, and my knees were shaking. I was so nervous that I could hardly speak... and that "audience" was my dog and a row of pillows that I had propped up and placed around the room so that I could practice presenting and giving eye contact to an audience. I imagined a room full of people, and that alone made my heart race. But knowing that in order to grow, I needed to "Feel the fear and do it anyway." This was my chance. I practiced and practiced until I was comfortable presenting to a few "real" people at a time, in person.

Several months later, when I was just getting comfortable presenting to a few people at a time, I attended my company's Global Convention. I was sitting in the audience with 15,000 people, listening to a top leader share her story. She encouraged everyone to make it a goal, to someday speak on stage and inspire thousands of people with your story. A flood of panic hit me, and I said to myself... "If that's what success means, NO WAY!" Fear of public speaking was at the tippy top of my "NEVER" list. At that moment, I could not see past my fear, or outside of my comfort zone, to what would be possible in my future.

At that convention, I realized that even though I had success in business and other areas of life, this was a completely new venture. I knew that if it was going to happen, it was up to me to figure this out. I became a student of the industry, learning as much as I could from books, audio trainings, and mentors. I was now on a wonderfully exciting journey that was growing me into the leader I needed to become to achieve the goals I was after.

I experienced a moderate amount of success in my first two companies, learning a lot along the way, but hadn't yet hit my full stride. I heard stories of people climbing the ranks to the top of their company with rapid speed. I wanted so badly for that to me, and as time went on, I was embarrassed that it was not my story to tell. I was not an overnight mega-success at the start, and I struggled with it. In fact, at one point, I nearly walked away from the entire industry after a few years because of it. I knew I had it in me to play bigger, but I got stuck playing small inside my comfort zone. After being frustrated long enough, I said to myself, "If someone else can achieve top ranks in their company… it's possible! Why not me?" I am most competitive with myself, and the desire to prove that I could do it fueled me forward.

I chalked every bit of the journey up as tuition as I worked to reach my dreams. I'd like to share a few valuable things I've learned along the way.

Our greatest fears are our greatest pathways to discovering our greatest purpose. By facing my anxiety, I built confidence in myself and opened up a world of possibilities. I truly believe that everyone was born with greatness inside of them, and it's simply a matter of tapping into that greatness by breaking through our limiting beliefs and growing our mindset.

Every one of us possesses two of the most powerful things on the planet… the human brain and the human heart. Mindset connects the two, making dreams become a reality. Your success in business will be in direct proportion to how much you believe in who you are and what it is that you do. Network Marketing is 10% Mechanics & 90% Mindset. Mindset is everything.

GROWTH is the only guarantee you'll have a better future. It's massively important. It's not an automatic process. It takes intention. I had to determine that I wasn't going to stay where I was and that I had something great inside of me that I needed to share with the world, but it started with personal growth. The truth is that it starts with personal growth with all of us.

Reading, listening to audio trainings, and attending events, have been key components to my success. Immersing myself in learning about the industry, the company, and the products have been massively important in understanding what it is that I have my hands on. It's an amazing career, and what it can do to change your life is incredible. But growing your skillset is also necessary, and that happens by one thing only, and that's by taking action. Action is what builds your paycheck.

Your ENVIRONMENT is also hugely important. People that you associate with have the biggest impact on who you are. If I had learned this in the beginning, I would have grown faster. You want to protect your environment fiercely from the negative people and the dream stealers that try to squash your dreams. We are designed to grow and thrive. Environment matters.

Have PROPER EXPECTATIONS. A friend and mentor of mine, Carrie Dickie, says it best… "*You're bad before you're good, and good before you're great.*" In order to have long-term success, you must have vision and long-term mindset. Go the distance and stay the course by having clear goals and your destination in sight. Let the journey… even the highs and lows, build character. Character builds mental toughness and grit, and that makes you stronger. Some of the strongest and most amazing people I know in my life are from this industry for those reasons.

Be COACHABLE, and stay hungry. Regardless of professional status or background, if you have a burning desire for more in life, and you're willing to put the time in to learn, you WILL succeed in Network Marketing! Master persistence and consistency and your life will never be the same.

Along the way, I learned the importance of finding a company that wasn't a trend but one that had great customer retention. It's hugely valuable if you want to build a long-term asset. My third and current company was a charm. I hit the elite ranks and the income I wanted in my first 22 months and earned each incentive trip in front of me. I'm now no longer watching the world go by. I'm living a life that I had only once dreamed of. This has given us a chance to get out and truly drink life in, more than we ever could before. I've grown from someone who was afraid to fly to being a World Traveler and loving it.

None of this would be possible without a team of extraordinary people. Helping people become all that they can be is rewarding beyond belief. I've discovered my true passion. When I sit back and think about what it is that we get to do, it's pretty amazing. Create your story. Help others see what's possible, and you'll change their life, and there's simply not a better feeling in the world.

It's your life, so DREAM!

If you could go back in time, when you started your first business in Network Marketing, and could start all over again, what would you do differently?

Dream BIG & launch strong, right out of the gate with massive action. It's harder to build slow than it is to build fast… and it's much more FUN!

———————————

Marilee Maricich was a traditional business owner caught on a "Hamster Wheel" of trading time for money when she found Network Marketing. Becoming a student of the industry, she's grown her business into a high-level success income. It's been a perfect fit for her passion for helping others to discover the greatness within themselves.

5

MARCY SCHACTER

My philosophy of life has been most influenced by the multiple entrepreneurial pursuits I have undertaken. In spite of "the good, the bad and in the ugly" that exist within the much-maligned network marketing industry, I believe it is one of the most ethical and sound business models out there, and it is one that pays you the value you actually bring to the marketplace and no more.

One of the first lessons I learned was the management of expectations, and that is vital for your emotional well-being. I go into every meeting with an open mind and no agenda except to learn how I might help this person in front of me. The second lesson was to adopt an attitude that I was already a leader before I even earned the rank. In other words, step up and be the one responsible for my success and not blame the company or others for my results. I also look to being part of the solution instead of complaining about the issues that come up in any business endeavour. The third and probably most important was to conquer my fears and drown out the "Dream-stealers who had no idea what I was truly embarking on anyway and especially as so many of these folks live in fear. I was on a path to change my financial future and improve the quality of life for myself and those who cared to join me whether they be a customer or a team member.

My credo was, "Have the fear and do it anyway!" Choosing to be your own boss means never knowing what is hiding around the next bend. The risks I took were so out of my comfort zone that is I needed a process that could keep me grounded. Years ago, I taught my acting students in my first business some of these techniques. My business then was a hybrid of personal development and performance training intended for anyone seeking to expand their creativity and blow through limiting beliefs. Picturing these beliefs as snowflakes amidst a storm, you could either whisk them away or be engulfed by them.

I always reminded my students, *"It is never safe to play safe!"* So many great accomplishments come with hard life lessons and staying in your comfort zone will never test you or help you become the human or the artist you are meant to be. You will inevitably suppress your brilliance and your creativity by "playing safe," whether it be in art, business or even love! Seek to conquer your fears so that that they no longer rule you. And lastly, learn to course-correct as quickly as possible. These two last principles have stood me well.

Over my 40 year plus entrepreneurial roller coaster ride, none of the missteps have taken me down- at least not for long. The hardest bumps delivered the most profound lessons and hence the greatest rewards. I have learned to master qualities of resilience, humour, compassion (for myself and others) in addition to self-appreciation and being as authentic as I can be in all areas of my life. Thankfully most of the above skills and mindsets can be cultivated and learned by anyone with a desire to do so. The keyword here being **"Desire."**

My First Aha -This came in 1992 when I recognized that even though I had grown in some areas, I was still playing safe. I was so afraid of others judging me- which I would not even look at these business opportunities. And when I joined my first company, I was too embarrassed to talk about the industry and to avoid the inevitable rejection I expected; I became a raving lunatic about my company's life-changing products. Of course, that was not well received either, but once that fear was identified, I knew what I had to do.

Where does the fear begin? In my case, I was a sensitive middle child, awkward and shy and thrust into a family of extroverts. My parents exuded extraordinary confidence and were admired for everything they accomplished. My siblings rolled through life, seemingly unburdened by fear and doubt. My eldest brother, a scholastic genius and athletic Ninja, was gorgeous and popular amongst his peers. My other brother made Paul Newman look like a slouch. Super funny, highly social and adventurous. Not only did all the girls adore him, but his friends also wanted to be him! My baby sister was funny, cute and was not plagued by the angst I experienced. It seemed as though everyone but me had figured out the way to shine and I was this dull and un-tested human who had to prove I was worthy. I had no belief that any of my ideas or opinions would be welcomed.

Then something happened that changed everything. It took years to take ownership of this, but I discovered that once I achieved clarity about what I wanted, I could leap out of my comfort zone and go after anything I desired.

This inner transformation began in grade five. I was voted the best actress by all my classmates- for real! Finally validated, I overcome the worst of all fears. The one that most people feel they would rather die than take on! Public speaking and performance. When I realized I had finally found my secret gift – I was lit up!

Fast forward 30 years, and my parents opened the door to the world of network marketing. Colleagues and friends had pursued me to join their "deal" – and I finally saw the light. It was the allure of true-time freedom and controlling my own destiny. Having become a daring renegade over the years with a focus on personal development, I was now ready to embrace the profession. **I see the industry now as "Personal Development with a paycheck!"**

Overcoming fears and doubts here took on a whole new meaning. I loved the idea of what in my film and T.V. acting years we called "Mailbox money." It meant coming home from my gruelling waitress job while pursuing a theatre career, that I'd find a sizeable check for a T.V. commercial I had done two years ago. The magic of "residual income" put me in the NETWORK MARKETING fast lane. I had to figure out the game, though and earn that same benefit without all the rejection that was in my acting profession. That was a joke, of course. Yet somehow, my acting career had prepared me, and I cared less about the rejections here because this career path didn't define me- It was simply a vehicle to get me somewhere I wanted to be.

I won recruits to my team and armed myself against the judgements of those who could not see what I saw. The poor fools, I thought. They have a job or, as we like to say, J.O.B., "just over broke." I felt I could lead these weary souls to the land of freedom, but no such thing. I had not yet learned to be "detached" from the outcome. People often remark, "I can see why you can do this – but not me, not ever!" I was way too invested in everyone joining me. I had to become "Ten Foot Tall and bulletproof!" I learned to use the word "next" and play the numbers game until eventually, those numbers led me to my "tribe." These individuals who wanted more from life than just a paycheck, and they were willing to go to the wall to achieve their "Why! I no longer "needed" them to join me. I had no attachment, and it was so freeing.

I was passionate yet still very rough and untrained in those early years, and I especially realized that the day I attended my company's convention in Anaheim, California, with over 5,000 of us. One of the late great Network Marketing mentors and multiple best-selling author, John Kalench, spoke, and there was a defining moment. I came away, finally able to understand the real work I was doing. Sorting for leaders and those who wanted more out of life. I thank Mr. Kalench for teaching me to treat this industry with the utmost respect it deserves.

Following that event, I invested into trainings with the likes of Bob Proctor, Jack Canfield, Zig Ziglar, Tony Robbins and a host of others. This built up my arsenal of knowledge and skills in manifesting what I wanted and helping others to do the same. Ultimately it is everyone's job to figure out their life purpose. I love the idea that we all have music in us. We just need to listen for it and begin to hum along until we know all the lyrics, finesse the melody and finally deliver the performance of our lifetime!

In summary, the biggest moments of learning:

1. Embracing my fear and doing it anyway.
2. Not caring what others think of me.

3. Learn compassion for myself and others. Come from your heart and be a servant leader to others, and you will never fail.

If you could go back in time when you started your first business in network marketing and you could start all over again, what would you do differently?

There is only one thing I would do differently if I could go back in time when I started my first network marketing business, and that is to quit managing my team and holding their hands- let them become independent and go find those that want this freedom lifestyle so bad they will never quit!

———————

Better to ask Marcy which career path she hasn't ventured into! A former actress, playwright, theatre director, gourmet foodie and culinary chef with a background in both business and the personal development industry, she's done it all. Having suffered a series of car accidents over a 20 year period, she hit the end of the road in 2008. With severe and chronic health issues, she spent the next six years searching for solutions doctors couldn't provide. One day a friend shared a product – and it actually worked! Since then, Marcy has dedicated herself to helping others. *"I'm so grateful for the opportunity afforded me in the network marketing industry which has led me to amazing friends around the globe and living a freedom lifestyle many would envy."*

Her mission is to empower others to do the same, giving them the choice to spend their time doing more of the things they love. This past year, since Covid, Marcy (known as the "ever ready bunny") has revelled in more "chill out" time, allowing her to recharge those overworked batteries and do more of her writing and painting. *"Most days do not feel like work as I would share what I know without a paycheck attached. But the residual income is awesome, and the bonus is partnering with a world-class team of like-minded dream-builders impacting the health and emotional wellbeing of people all over the world."*

6

VALERIE ALOISIO

It is often said that through life's tragedies, we experience our greatest blessings. I am sure many of you can relate to those times in your life – those defining moments – when you just know that something has got to change, something is just not "right", whatever "that" may be. This journey for me occurred over 27 years ago when I lost my mother, my best friend, to breast cancer. She was only 59, way too young. I was pregnant with my daughter and had a three-year-old son at the time. Obviously, for me, this was a defining moment. I realized that life is precious, and we can't take anything for granted. A few years later, another defining moment... divorce. This experience led to some health challenges; depression, anxiety, insomnia, a feeling of worthlessness, and I had a hard time dealing with it all. It was a dark time in my life; something I had never imagined would happen to me. I prayed for help, anything that could help me get my life back. I'm sure many can relate to those life changes that happen that just rock your world. And then another defining moment. I was introduced to network marketing by a dear friend. She shared her products, which helped me. But more importantly, she introduced me to the world of personal growth and development and mindset and incredible mentors that helped me overcome the challenges I was facing at the time. This was indeed life-changing for me, which is why I am so passionate about network marketing!

This was 20 years ago, and I almost missed the opportunity. I had a college degree and a successful career in corporate America and thought that having a job was the only responsible way one could raise a family. It was indeed stressful at times juggling so many things, but that was life. However, as we talked more about the opportunity, I could see that perhaps work/life balance and better quality of life for my children and me was indeed possible. I had no experience in sales and zero belief in myself at that time, so I said, "No, thank you, I'll refer people to you." And then another defining moment occurred when she replied, "You've been complaining about not having any balance in your life, and yet you won't even look at this." And then her next few words changed my life: "A closed mind is a wonderful thing to lose." That was a wake-up call for me and one that just made sense. So, I took a leap of faith and started my network marketing business and never looked back.

There were five simple things I was looking for in an opportunity.

1) There was truly no limit to what I could earn,
2) My income would directly relate to the amount of effort I put into it,
3) I could build a passive, residual income stream that would give me the quality of life I was looking for,
4) The mission and vision of the company matched my values, and
5) I could make a difference in other people's lives.

I made the decision to become a professional network marketer and an entrepreneur and immersed myself in the education and training necessary to achieve success. Success was the only option, and I jumped "all in." I didn't know how this was going to happen. I knew that if I put in the proper effort and attitude and learn from those that succeeded before me, then I could make it happen. I just had to do this – failure was not an option. Within 18 months, I replaced my prior income and never looked back. I always tell others that you don't have to know the "how"; the "how" will present itself. You must want it badly enough and be hungry for whatever change you want to see in your life.

Taking that leap of faith was truly worth it. It wasn't always easy. I wanted to quit. But then I remembered my "why', what I had been through, and my children. I am not the same person I was 20 years ago. Today, I am an entrepreneur and successful businesswoman with a global business, all as a result of helping other people either physically or financially get what they want. I was able to purchase a nice home for my family, travel to some amazing places around the world and created a wonderful lifestyle. I worked my business around my children's schedules and was always there for them. They were my priority, but they also knew my business was important to me and to our future. They developed a great deal of respect for what I was doing. I shared with them the lessons I was learning not only in business but in personal growth. Today my children have received their university degrees, have their own apartments in NYC, are gainfully employed in their chosen profession and doing extremely well. I am very proud of them.

It has been my mission since I chose network marketing as my career to professionalize this industry and to always share it with others so that they can have the work/life balance and the financial stability and eventual financial independence that many only dream of. The fact that one can have their own home-based business, be mentored by others, and be part of a community that encourages growth and the proper mindset for success is what is so exciting to me! I am now able to add value, give back, and "pay it forward" today in a way I never imagined. I am a hands-on leader who encourages independence and growth. It is so rewarding to help others realize their dreams and goals, and this industry provides the vehicle to do so; and for that, I am very grateful!

Please be aware that this industry of network marketing and working with people will challenge your patience level. You must be patient. You can only control your actions and reactions, not other people's actions/reactions or lack thereof. As I share the following success tips, always remember that patience is a virtue and keep this top of mind.

1. Be the best version of YOU. It is all about mindset and personal development as a human being. This is not taught in a traditional school. I truly believe this is "everything." I am a better person today because of network marketing and being exposed to the world of personal development and mastering your mind, and I feel blessed to have been mentored by some of the best in this industry.

2. Follow the leader. Allow yourself to be mentored by those who have what you want and are the kind of person you want to emulate. Follow the system in place. Do not reinvent the wheel, however, put your personality out there. People join people that care, so check your attitude and your posture. We are in the people business, and this is not always easy. We have a volunteer army in network marketing. A mentor told me, "You can't fix lazy, you can't fix stupid, and you can't push a

string!" Look for people that are entrepreneurial, passionate, hard-working, proud and kind. This will make your life a lot easier in this profession.

3. Network marketing is about putting in the time and effort that is relevant for the lifestyle you want to have. Only you can decide what that is. Be open and coachable. I almost missed this because I wasn't open to listening and learning something new (network marketing). Be choosy with whom you work and with whom you associate. Negative nellies must be left behind. Set goals and achieve them. It's about the small wins that lead you to success. Just don't quit. Know WHY you are doing this business. And it must be more than just money.

4. Make a decision, step outside of your comfort zone and go for it! It's worth the journey.

If you could go back in time when you started your first business in network marketing and you could start all over again, what would you do differently?

When I began my network marketing career, I was extremely product-focused, and I thought I had to become an expert in the products. It took me a while to learn to become a student of the process, the fundamentals of network marketing, and the compensation plan. My passion and excitement in the early days compensated for the lack of business experience, and I did make money. But I hit a plateau, and that is when I sought mentorship to figure out why. I was told that I had to focus on my mindset as well as the process and become a student of network marketing and leadership development. I took that advice seriously, became a student of the industry, and my business took off.

Lifestyle Business Entrepreneur, Mentor, Contributing Author, Speaker and World Traveler.

My core values of integrity, family, faith, and making a difference are everything to me. Corporate career in Human Resources and Training & Development. Introduced to network marketing 20 years ago, specializing in leadership development.

7

BRENDA LEE GALLATIN

My love for this industry started at a very young age. I was six or seven when my friend Sandy and I set up a lemonade stand on the dirt sidewalk in front of our salt-box house. I see it and feel it in my mind even after all these years. Warm sunny day, the fragrant smell of freshly cut grass just inside the rock wall (so common in New England), and the waft of lilacs from the gentle warm breeze. The table was covered with a pretty yellow flower print cloth, the lovely lapis blue pitcher, and assorted color cups from Mom's Fiesta Ware. My crazy, very boisterous yellow-headed Mexican parrot was outside in her cage on her own rickety table by the steps where Mom placed her on warm days. When folks stopped by, she would be all excited and agitated, loudly screaming over and over, "Doffy, Doffy, HELP!" My mom's name was Dorothy, and that was as close as Polly could say her name.

Let me not leave out Midgie. My constant companion was a black and white terrier who happily, tail wagging, welcomed our guests to the lemonade stand.

We were two little girls giddy with excitement waving people to stop and enjoy a refreshing lemonade. When the lemonade was all gone, we split the money and trotted straight for the Apothecary (General Store) to spend it all on penny candy.

Who knew the Entrepreneur bug bit way back then!

I was a spunky-spirited, independent girl full of vim, vigor, and talent. I was the one chosen for the lead roles in the school play. I was the one chosen to sing the solo at school celebrations. I was the "lil' darling" who did her miniature song and tap dance routine at the annual community minstrel show – loving the excitement and costumes and applause while being oblivious to the pain taking root and festering somewhere deep inside.

Unbeknownst to me, my invisible, unidentified pain began to manifest in a myriad of ways, with my behavior becoming an issue. Soon I was labeled "delinquent!" Spent a fair amount of time in the principal's office, and getting expelled became a common experience.

My parents divorced when I was five years old, leaving me with lasting unidentified pain. Much later, I learned I am a survivor of Domestic Violence and Alcoholism. I learned my rebellious behavior was not about being a "bad" person, but a manifestation of my undealt-with pain.

Why would I include this in my chapter? Because many of you are dragging along pain from your childhood and haven't identified its effect on why you think and do like you do. There may be some hidden blocks keeping you spinning around and around getting nowhere – or getting great traction and success only to unintentionally sabotage your efforts.

For now, suffice to say from age five on, I pretty much had to fend for myself. The details are a story for another book.

That spunky-spirited lil' girl is still in there all these years later; however, that wonderful sparkle and spunky spirit now serves and manifests in a myriad of wonderful ways.

I met my husband thru a blind date when I was almost 15. I told him I was 18. He believed me. He was in the Navy, stationed in Newport, Rhode Island. Something about that gorgeous Navy Uniform was magical!!!!

We married when I was 16. At 17, we moved from Massachusetts to his hometown in Minnesota with one and a half babies in tow.

As a young couple with little money, trying to set up our home, I would sign up with different companies to take advantage of a discount – certainly not understanding anything about network marketing, direct sales, or team building. Whether I wanted laundry soap or candles, vitamins or distilled water, encyclopedias or wigs, makeup or jewelry, I would sign up and enthusiastically (and naively) tell my friends and anyone else I met about whatever the wonderful thing I was using and, surely, they would want it, too! I made a little money along the way.

If I only knew then what I learned later about network marketing.

I was 25 and pregnant with my fifth child of six when I really wanted and needed some containers for my kitchen. So, of course, I signed up with a company. My sponsor taught me to "build a team." Voila! This was my first experience of being mentored in this business. When the boxes of containers arrived, the kids and I would put the orders together, then joyfully pack all the boxes and our bodies into the car to go make deliveries! Can you visualize the scene? BTW I still have my original yellow, avocado, and orange canisters!

In just three months with this company, I earned my first car in this industry. What a blessing with perfect timing! We needed a car sooo badly! My mom passed away during that time, and we needed a way to transport her remains back to Massachusetts for burial. We enjoyed the trip in our beautiful, brand new, light blue, air-conditioned (big deal then!) station wagon. Who knew?

During these years, with a very busy life around five kids, I went back to school. I had to finish high school by getting my GED, but then went on to get a Bachelor's degree and kept going to finish my Master's a few years later. And decided to accumulate several specialty certifications since then.

I may not have been the highly favored student in Jr High, being expelled over and over for every little infraction, but as I matured, I became a lover of learning. I will continue to be a lifelong student 'til I'm "in my box." I thirst for anything to do with psychology, personal development. Mindset, coaching, network marketing. I love it all!

Throughout my life, regardless of circumstances, I've had one foot in a network marketing company. I love the industry! The freedom, the fun, the relationships, achievements, recognition, awards, prizes, trips, cars, and independence ... and the income! Being an employee, having to punch a time clock, get up before 10 am, one or two quick potty breaks and 45 minutes for lunch, minimum wage, and – are you kidding me?! – ONE week of vacation? Mercy!!!!! Not my style. I know – I tried it a few times.

Because life was so full with five kids (plus foster kids), a farm, my business adventures, college and a husband who always worked two or three jobs to keep us well fed, the stress was too much. Our marriage hit a breaking point, and we nearly divorced ten years in. Remember this spunky, feisty, strong-willed, immature brat child was now a wife, mom, homemaker, and businesswoman. Yes, Jim is a saint!

It was our pastor who helped us through that season. Jim and I got on our knees and surrendered our marriage to the Lord.

OH BOY! Here comes the next big chapter in our life. We both simultaneously felt called to make a leap and commit to a life of ministry. At age 33, Jim enrolled in seminary while continuing his full-time job. That meant he left us on Monday and returned on Friday. This went on for a couple years. I also attended classes at the seminary. This was a true test – we passed it! So now I had a new title: "Pastor Jim's wife."

Fast forward to our second church assignment, and I'm pregnant with our sixth child. (We ultimately ended up with five sons and a daughter). One day a couple of guys knocked on my door. They were selling encyclopedias. This was when "cold calling" was "door-to-door" sales. Their demo was so appealing I started to cry because I wanted the books so badly for my kids. I could not afford to spend that amount of money and had to say no. A few days later, they returned to tell me they had a plan for me to get the encyclopedias. If I could sell three sets, I would earn a set for free. I was all over that offer! Of course, I could do that! I had a hot burning desire!

Visiting door-to-door in my neighborhood, I sold encyclopedias like hotcakes.

At a local meeting for the company, I was invited to the front of the room and, to my complete surprise, was recognized as having sold more CEP'S than anyone in the region. I whispered to the guy, "I don't know what a CEP is!?" You see, CEP stands for "complete educational program." I did not know you could sell the encyclopedia, the Cyclo Teacher, and the children's books separately – so every sale I made was for the whole enchilada! Sometimes it's really beneficial if you don't know you can break up sets and sell just onesies. I still have the beautiful crystal pitcher and clock radios I earned along with memories from a trip for two to Rosario in the San Juan Islands.

There were many other network marketing ventures to follow. I just wish I knew sooner what I didn't know! Network marketing has gotten a bad rap in the past. I am here to tell you it is a very honorable profession. Don't listen to any negative comments. Remember, your naysayers don't pay your bills! They just don't know! Just like I did not know!

If I knew then what I know now, I would have jumped into this industry as a serious career path much sooner, rather than it just being a fun thing to do to get a discount. I did astonishingly well for not knowing the benefit and skill of team building and treating it like the serious business it truly is.

My enthusiasm, excitement, and belief for the product and company I was "currently" enjoying took me to heights I never even knew were possible.

Now, after over 50 years in and out of this industry alongside raising six kids, going to school, having a private counseling practice specializing in Marriage, Family, Domestic Violence and Addiction, and being a busy Pastor's wife with a myriad of responsibilities, I found myself in 2012 at age 69 saying "YES" one more time.

Jim and I were concerned about how we would make it until we are "in our boxes" on Social Security. I would joke and say, "Oh, Honey, that's why we had six kids. No worries! We can stay two months with each and repeat." I was trying to make light of a very serious concern.

We prayed about this, and three days later, our answer was delivered. The company I had always dreamed of I found at a Woman's Show booth.

Who knew? God knew!!!

It was at this time, Jim was diagnosed with Parkinson's. They said he probably had it 10-12 years already. We didn't know. Yes. It is a progressive, declining disease.

I include this part of my story to tell you, once again, this network marketing "thing" is the real deal and a wonderful gift for anyone who will receive it – and DO IT! The fruit of my labor is providing us with the ability to provide the things that make life a little easier for us, such as a beautiful mobility van, wheelchairs, walkers, scooters, and the medical and naturopathic services insurance doesn't cover.

I wake up and go to bed every day filled with gratitude for God delivering this business to me. I am so grateful for each and every business partner and customer. Each individual is an integral member of our extended family. Together we soar!

I want to share with you a few "pro tips" I have learned along the way to help you on your journey to greatness in network marketing.

Ready?

Choose something you are PASSIONATE about. What brings you joy? What lights you up? And make sure it's consumable to ensure monthly repeat orders!

Just say YES! Don't overthink it! Do not put it off! Say YES and earn as you learn. Do not think you have to know it all or the "right" way to do it ... JUST DO IT!

Mind Your Mind!!!! Invest in your mind! I believe everything hinges on your mindset, and it takes intentional effort to cultivate and grow a healthy mindset. I know I have given way too much time and power to the monkey in my mind whispering negative messages stemming all way back to my childhood. Being straight-up honest with you, that old monkey still likes to visit from time to time. Monkey reminds me, *"I'm not good enough,"* *"I'm not smart enough,"* *"remember when you left school in tenth grade you were labeled as least likely to succeed"*, *"you are a fraud,"* *"you can't,"* *"you are a loser,"* *"give it up – you'll never succeed"* ... you get the idea? We carry around with us old life commandments we swallowed hook, line, and sinker and are imbedded in our psyche in childhood without being aware of the lifetime effect. Deeply internalized messages. Ever heard, *"kids are to be seen and not heard?"* *How might that affect your voice?* *"You are a troublemaker,"* *"don't talk to strangers,"* etc. Get it? Curiously enough, from time to time, we fall into stinkin' thinkin' which has its roots from childhood. Spend the time and money to work on personal development. It can only benefit.

Be curious. Read, read, read, and read some more! Attend classes and sign up for courses on personal development. I have so many to recommend and have been so blessed to be mentored by so many wonderful thought leaders.

Be coachable and open to instruction from your leaders who have walked the path before you!

Follow the proven system! IT WORKS IF YOU WORK IT!!!!!!

Commit to stick and stay! Remember, QUITTERS NEVER WIN, AND WINNERS NEVER QUIT!!!!!

My secret sauce has been described as loving, unstoppable, enthusiastic, passionate, spunky, spirited, fun, creative, loyal, and inspiring encourager!

I am on the other end of this journey now at age 77, but I am still fully engaged and have another amazing chapter in me ... I hope it's a long one!

I am called to be a catalyst in my mission to *Make People Better*. I hope on my dash it will say, "*She Made People Better*."

If you could go back in time when you started your first business in network marketing and you could start all over again, what would you do differently?

I would take this industry of network marketing as a very serious business and career path – as indeed it IS!

I would be more coachable and follow the proven system rather than thinking, "I've got this!"

———

Entrepreneur Extraordinaire, Author, Speaker, Coach, Trainer & Network Marketer, Brenda Lee has been in Network Marketing for over 50 years, alongside being a busy Pastor's wife, raising one daughter and five sons and having a private counseling practice specializing in Marriage, Family, Domestic Violence and Addiction she is now retired from.

Brenda Lee has a genuine passion for life, an incredible contagious energy and a huge heart of gold. Her life mission is truly to *Make People Better.*

8

KATHY HENKEN

In 1996, I attended a product party that a friend of mine hosted. I really enjoyed the products and the person that did the demonstration. When she shared with the guests that booking a party would not only help our host earn gifts but give us free products too, I signed up to host one myself. That one party turned into three over the course of the next 18 months. However, not once during those parties did the representative approach me about doing the business. I didn't think anything of it. I was unaware of the Network Marketing Industry. No one in my family nor anyone I knew was in this profession. Well, if you don't count the lady down the street from us when I was a child. She used to give us miniature white tubes of lipstick for our dolls. Does that ring a bell with anyone?

Almost a decade later, I was helping a friend work her booth of homemade goods at a holiday bazaar. The person in the booth next to us had a lot of people interested in her products. I watched as her calendar filled up rapidly with appointments. Curiosity led me to start asking her questions, and we met for coffee several days later. It was with her and the company she was partnered with that I began my Network Marketing career.

At that time, I had two young daughters and had a corporate job where I worked long hours and traveled several times a month. I knew it put a strain on our family, so the possibility of building a business of my own that allowed me to stay home and replace my income was so exciting! A year later, I was able to quit my full-time job. However, five years after enrolling, that company went bankrupt. It was unexpected, and I didn't have a backup plan. Over the next several years, I enrolled with three other companies but never felt I got in my groove with them.

Let me ask you several questions.

- Have you known someone that had to choose which utility bill to pay because they could only pay one?

- How about someone that had to hide their car because it was on the hit list to be repossessed?

- Have you ever known anyone whose home was in foreclosure?

Then you knew me.

In 2006, we had become small traditional business owners, and the financial crisis of 2008 hit us hard. Everything came to a screeching halt. We depleted our retirement funds to try to keep the business afloat. I had gone back into the workforce and was working four traditional jobs. From the outside, everything looked the same. No one knew our kids were on free lunch programs. They didn't know I was hiding my car to keep it from being taken by the bank, and we were running up credit card debt to pay monthly living expenses.

Even though I knew the challenges weren't specific to us, and many others were having the same struggle, I wore a shroud of shame. I swear, all my clothing was black in color... and they had hoods.

One afternoon I received a call from someone I hadn't seen in over a year. She didn't know what was happening in my life. She called to ask if I had a couple of minutes so she could share something she was excited about. A product with results she loved sold through a network marketing company she loved even more. She wanted to know if she sent me information about the product and the company if I would look at it. "Sure," I said. But in my head, I was thinking, "I don't have the money to purchase what she's offering." When I opened the box and looked through the business information, something changed in my head. WHAT IF this is what we've been praying for? WHAT IF this could change our situation? WHAT IF this was the box of hope? The WHAT IF changed to WHY NOT?

My desire, willingness to work and coachability gave me the confidence to step off and start running right away. It meant making more sacrifices. But, I finally felt like the sacrifices I was making were for my family, not for my employers' families. I was exposed to personal development in my corporate career by a mentor, not the corporation. I recognized how important it was, especially in this profession, and I started reading and listening to as many books as I was able. I showed up for everything. Every meeting, every training, and every call. It was the best way for me to learn from those having the success I wanted. I found mentors along the way. I believe there are few industries like Network Marketing where people are so willing to help others succeed.

There are many activities that, when done together, will create momentum in your business. These are the ones I consider to be at the top.

- Be wildly curious about others. Learn to ask questions. People will tell you a lot about themselves when they know you care about getting to know them. It's much easier to be a solution provider when you understand someone's needs.

- Ask, without judgement, if they will accept your offer to share what you have with them. Think of it like this… If you have a plate full of the best cookies ever made and you're in a room full of people, you offer the cookies to everyone. You don't decide who wouldn't or shouldn't have a cookie. And when they say "No," you don't try to force them to take the cookie; you move to the next person. But the next time you have cookies, you ask again. And you keep asking. So many successful people in this profession were asked multiple times, over a long period of time, by the same person before they said yes to enrolling. Timing is everything. When someone says "no" to my offer, I always ask, "Does no means no, not right now or does it mean no, I'd rather chew glass?" Have a sense of humor and a good attitude. If they say "No means not right now." ask for their permission to follow up with them later.

- Follow up! Follow up! Follow up! It's said the fortune is in the follow-up. It's an activity that creates success in most things. Our book of business depends on us sharing with people and following up with those we have.

I am so happy I said "yes" to the person that shared with me, and I'll be forever grateful to her. The success I've had with the company I joined has changed my life, my family's lives and the thousands of customers and business partners in my organization. I have met incredible people, traveled to amazing places and have time freedom that allows me to spend my days doing what fulfills me. All because someone asked me to look at what they have to offer. I am surrounded with positive people that are able to help others look, feel and live better.

If you could go back in time when you started your first business in network marketing and you could start all over again, what would you do differently?

I would ask MORE people FASTER! I was fearful in the beginning that people would judge me, so I didn't ask as many people as I should have. Follow a business model that creates duplicity and empowers others.

Kathy grew up in Seattle, Washington. The oldest of seven children, she attributes her strengths and weaknesses to her birth order. She is an extrovert who considers one of her strengths to be her interpersonal skills, where she finds herself meeting new people and learning new things, which she thoroughly enjoys. She loves to travel, watch movies, play games, cook and spend time with her family and friends or a combination thereof. She and her husband Doug have been married 26 years and are adjusting to their empty nest life. They recently moved to Boise, ID, to be near their beautiful daughters, Taylor and Madison and their families because, if honest, the empty nest life isn't going so well.

9

SAIREEN NEILSEN

My Mom and Dad were very inspirational to me. They were born in Fiji, as was I. There were ten children in my Dad's family and nine children in my Mom's family. My Dad was only able to get a grade seven education because his family couldn't afford to pay for further schooling, and he was pulled out of school to work for his family in the sugarcane fields. He is a smart man, though. He taught himself and became a police officer in Fiji. My Mom was an assistant to a school teacher. They left their families, and they emigrated from Fiji to Vancouver in pursuit of the Canadian Dream, to provide a better life for themselves and their two little girls, and I appreciate their sacrifice.

When my older sister and I came to Vancouver, she was eight, I was five, and we didn't speak any English. However, in grade one, I won an award for the most improved student, in grade seven, I was the House President, and in grade twelve, I was the Grade Twelve Vice President of Student Council.

From these experiences, I learned to always be fair, empathetic, compassionate, helpful, genuine, kind, generous, and fun. I discovered that I had a natural ability to lead and help others. My past experiences helped mould and shape the person I am today. Oh yes, and I learned always to say please and thank you!

I worked several jobs while still in school. I once took a job selling vacuum cleaners. I sold a total of one vacuum cleaner – to my parents—such lovely people.

Eventually, I worked in a few women's retail clothing stores, and I was always a top salesperson. An important lesson that I eventually applied to network marketing was to be truthful. If something looked terrible on a customer, I would tell them. I wouldn't make the sale, but I'd build trust and a relationship, and those same customers would come back to me and buy more than if I'd tried to sell them something that wasn't right for them.

I was introduced to my network marketing company through a friend of a friend, Dave. I started off trying the products as an alternative to some of the medication I was taking. I wanted a more holistic approach to my health. I took the products and, over time, started noticing a difference.

I learned a bit more about the network marketing company at a time when I was somewhat dissatisfied and unhappy with my employment situation. At the time, I was working at a dental practice. I realized that I wanted to work for myself and work on my terms. I didn't want to have to beg for a raise, have someone else assess my performance and essentially have my employer define my self-worth.

I loved the idea of working together with like-minded people, including several mentors, on a common goal. I loved the idea of being paid weekly based on my own efforts and those of our team as well. I loved the idea of having self-development opportunities.

It was also important to me to find a business platform that did not discriminate against a person's age, skin colour, gender, ethnic background or whether one spoke English well.

In the beginning, when I started with the network marketing company, I thought it would be easy. Since I was a top salesperson in retail, I thought it would not be difficult to sell these new products that I loved so much.

I soon questioned whether the sales techniques utilized in the retail environment were transferrable to the new environment. I was not getting the results that I wanted, and I was hardly achieving my weekly goals. In retail, people would come in to see me. In network marketing, I had to go out and meet people.

Even though I enjoyed meeting people, it wasn't transferring into sales success. I was pushing my own sales agenda, wasn't asking the right questions and wasn't listening to my client's needs. I was selling, not sharing, which turned some people off.

If I asked someone about their interest in the products offered by my business, and they indicated that they were not interested, I used to agonize over what I'd said or hadn't said. I created so many stories about a conversation when I heard a "no," and that sometimes led me to start thinking negatively.

My inner voice would be saying things like, "I can't do this; I don't know everything I should; maybe if I knew everything, then I could answer more questions for the prospect," and that would lead my inner voice to ask the big one, "Why are other people more successful in the business than I am?" I found my energy and enthusiasm were deflating. I was getting discouraged and wanted to quit.

When I recognized that my initial approach wasn't working, I knew it was time to do things differently in order to get different results. It was up to me to take responsibility for my own actions and results. I realized that I needed to put in the time to: learn what worked and didn't work; develop my skill sets to enhance my confidence; get out of my comfort zone; consider my strengths and weaknesses, and grow. I needed to become the person I wanted to be.

Essentially, I needed to grow into being a leader, and I learned that as a confident leader, I should not be afraid to say, "That's a very good question. I don't have the answer right now, but I will get back to you." That removed a lot of self-induced stress.

I read books, I went to seminars and workshops, and I went to conventions. I surrounded myself with successful mentors. I even joined a group that focused on how to do business by listening to your heart (heart-led).

Instead of selling, I had to change the way I showed up with these products. I considered the products and the business opportunity to be beautiful gifts that were meant to be shared with as many people as possible. I stopped selling and started sharing those gifts in order to make a difference in people's lives.

I think the three primary tips that created my success are:

• Be an active listener;

• Help people to get what they want; and

• Be authentic and heart-led.

Remember, when I said that I was questioning why the sales techniques I had successfully applied in retail sales didn't work in the network marketing environment? Well, they do apply; I just wasn't applying them properly.

In retail, I listened to what my customers wanted, and I was truthful as to whether the outfit they tried on was well suited to what they wanted. I was actively listening; I was helping people get what they wanted, and I was authentic.

In my network marketing role, initially, I wasn't actively listening to my prospects or asking the right questions, and because of that, I didn't know what they really wanted or needed.

I started being an active listener, focusing on my customer's needs and considering how I could help them. I got to know people better. We might talk about someone's health or a business opportunity, but it was often good to just share a kind word and a smile. There are so many ways to help or make a difference in people's lives. It's not all about doing the business.

When I have a new customer or a new business partner, I do something extra nice for them as it makes it more personal and helps develop the relationship. Just as I listen and ask questions regarding their needs, I find out what they like in their personal lives as well. That is my authentic self.

Active listening for a business prospect means that I write down the prospect's goals and determine how we can realistically work together to reach those goals and help them get what they want.

I figured out that customers and potential business partners are best served by learning about the products and business in a way that works for them. Not everyone learns the same way. Some people are more visual. Some people like to listen to podcasts or watch videos or read a book that inspires them. You can guide them on that.

I had to get better at making presentations to customers and potential business partners. Ultimately, the only way that worked was to make presentations in my own way and not compare my approach to others. While I admire the way my mentors and associates might do a presentation, I found that their approach often just didn't work for me.

I travel a fair amount globally with my husband for his business and our holidays, and, as a result, I have made amazing friendships and built relationships around the world. When I get off a plane, I set my intentions and ask myself how I can make a difference to the people I am meant to attract and help? I start off with the best of intentions for everyone.

I also learned not to take rejection or objections personally. I've come to realize that it simply might not be the right time for the person to whom I am presenting an opportunity, and, in fact, it's ok to ask for permission to check back with them sometime later. I've learned to move forward and try my best to stay positive every day.

All this work and change in my approach paid off. I attained a recognized sales level designation and an award from the network marketing company I am associated with, displaying an exceptional energy level and sustained active involvement in the business. I was quite proud of that.

Also, if anyone told me that in 2020 I would be jointly hosting a Facebook talk show and that I would be asked to contribute to a book on network marketing written by twenty powerful women, I wouldn't have believed them.

At least these accomplishments serve to confirm that I didn't peak in grade one.

It's funny that I was asked to share my story because I often say, "If I only knew my story." In fact, I know my story, but I've always been afraid to share it because: I thought I might get it wrong in the telling; there have been wins and failures along the way; I was afraid of being judged. Having said that, I am grateful for the opportunity to be part of this book as I am very inspired by the organizers and contributors to the book.

Writing this chapter required a bit of introspection, and I found that there are still some things to learn about myself. In trying to figure out "my story" in the context of this book, I had to give some thought to how I would measure the success I've had as I think it says a lot about me.

Some people measure success by how much money they have or when they achieve a certain level of status within their organization, and I've done fairly well by that measure. However, for me, it is more about helping people during my journey – being kind, being supportive, being an active listener, being compassionate, making people laugh, helping people get healthier, and assisting people in earning money. When I wake up in the morning, I pray that I can help people from a place of best intentions for everyone. My goal is to help people achieve their goals, bring out the best in them and help them shine. Achieving that goal is the true measure of my success.

I have developed these qualities over time and not overnight. I sometimes forget that I am this person because, like other women, we give and support our family and friends, and we forget to acknowledge how much we have grown, developed, and gained wisdom. We forget to celebrate our accomplishments. It's so easy to reflect on our failures to the point of paralyzing ourselves and disguising that as our comfort zone. We are such beautiful gifts to the world as we constantly grow and shift and become powerful influencers. We are so much more than a mother, daughter or wife. We are who we choose to be.

If you could go back in time and were just starting your first business in direct sales and you could start all over again, what would you do differently?

I would focus on sharing my knowledge. I would listen and learn. I would ask the right questions. I would not take objections or rejection personally. I would be my authentic self and try to make a difference in people's lives. I would stay positive. I would look for inspiration and try to inspire others. Oh, and I would not sell an expensive vacuum cleaner to my lovely parents.

———————

Saireen is a Vancouver based entrepreneur who has partnered with a global Network Marketing company. She is a beautiful and caring wife to her wonderful husband. Saireen jointly hosts a Facebook talk show, *Healthy Way Vibes*. She is very focused on giving back to the community.

10

LISA GROSSMANN

THE BEGINNING

My introduction to network marketing is a classic story. A relative called me and told me she **had** to come show me something that was going to make a fortune and was the greatest thing since sliced bread. She came to my house, took apart my sink, and hooked up a water filter product. I thought I was just trying it out to buy it. Little did I know that it was the beginning of three decades of wonderful insanity.

MY JOURNEY

My journey began with me thinking network marketing was interesting, and through the years helped form my belief that this was an opportunity to change the world in this space – to mentor, teach, and counsel others to create an income and a life they'd never imagined. To do for others. Give to others. Make a difference to others. And what a journey it's been.

My network marketing career can be divided into three decades. I was successful in the traditional world, but it was a family business, which was not fun for me. I discovered that even when you win the rat race, you're still a rat. So, network marketing was a kind of welcomed escape. I made no money for the first couple of years, but I didn't lose any either. I got a valuable education learning the business of network marketing. After a couple of years, I'd replaced my traditional income.

The family business that I hated so much was the gift that kept on giving. After we left the business, it came back to haunt us. The company had issues with the federal government, and the government wanted me to testify against my mother. I wasn't going to do that. My husband then got pulled into it. In the end, I cut a deal and spent 12 months and 12 days in a federal prison camp so my family wouldn't bear the brunt. After that experience, I wasn't the most employable person in the world, and network marketing was very forgiving. I came back into network marketing out of desperation with nowhere else to go. While I knew how to build a network marketing business, my greater strength was my understanding of the business of network marketing. So, initially, I consulted for friends, and if you've ever consulted for friends, you know you are basically doing it for free. I then decided to go with one of the companies that I had been consulting for and started building in 2001, where I established myself as a thought leader within the space. I earned five times what I earned per year in the first decade, and I sure didn't believe I was five times better. I didn't know if I was even two times better. I did have a different vantage point. I had a different work ethic. And my perspective was evolving. This part of my journey took me all over the world, including Asia, where I lived off and on for 15 years.

In the third decade, I sort of retired from the field. I still had a strong residual income from the last business that I built, which I still maintain today. I again started consulting, teaching, training, helping companies open, and assisting corporate teams overseas. While consulting was much more profitable the second time around, there was no opportunity for residual income, no earnings beyond the time on the clock. About three years ago, the people I'd worked with for many years were having great success with a product that I was so excited about that I wanted to be a customer. This company had a model that was so different than what I was used to. This was the company I had dreamed of for 30 years. It was the manifestation of what I thought the space could be. After three months of being a customer, I decided to dive in and go build again. Everything I'd done before, along with the years of experience gained overseas, came together during these past 3 years. I was able to build an amazing sustainable income, helped others realize their dreams, and delighted in seeing some that I'd mentored experience huge successes.

My journey has been an amazing one. We are a volunteer army; anybody can join and grow a business here. There's nothing quite like it. The money can be great, but having the chance to touch people's lives and have a hand in their successes are so much greater.

CHALLENGES AND ACCOMPLISHMENTS

My challenges are basically the same as everybody else's. I tend to have imposter syndrome – because I achieved a certain level in this business, I sometimes feel that I'm not quite as good as people think I am. Achievements, though, are really a function of the team of people you're working with. Nobody can do it by themselves. This is a very interdependent business. It's about growth and positive thinking and tenacity and belief transferred to others collectively.

There's also the struggle of wanting success more for people than they want it for themselves. Walking the line between enabling people and empowering them can be problematic. You want to help, but you find that you're doing too much for them. I guess that goes back to wanting more for someone than they want for themselves.

I went through some battles that were really in my head after the prison experience. One thing I love about network marketing is it's the most forgiving business. It doesn't care where you come from. Your age, gender or education. It only cares what you bring to the table and what you're willing to do. That was a struggle for me in the beginning because people can judge you without knowing you. But ignoring those people and staying true to yourself can give you more time and energy to find the ones who are positive. There are so many people in the world who need an opportunity. So many people that need our products. So many people that we haven't yet reached.

While I have worked very hard, I've also been very fortunate. I've consulted, helped start companies, taught and trained all over the world, and spoken on some of the most important industry stages. I've done very well in the space, but here's the takeaway: I'm 58 years old. I'm not particularly good at social media, and I'm worse at technology. And I'm at the top of my game. I'm still breaking my own records, achieving more, and reaching more people. To me, that speaks to the space – that speaks to the possibility and potential of network marketing. I am happier than I've ever been and more excited than I've ever been because the biggest success in my life is the overabundance of awesome people that I have in my life.

Over the years, I have received many accolades and spoken from the stage to tens of thousands of people over time. I've been the top earner in my company for a couple of years. But here's the true triumph: I'm happy to say that I am probably not the top earner today because I'm enrolling and supporting the next generation, particularly a young phenom who is better than I will ever be. And that's the beauty of success – you can attract people that want your mentorship, your institutional memory, and the knowledge wrapped up in your longevity. They're as good at what they do as you are at what you do, so it's an opportunity to mentor people who are also teaching you, and that's a tremendous success.

WHO I AM / PRICELESS ATTRIBUTES

I would describe myself as a contributor. A connector. And a thought leader. I'm the Chief Imagination Officer, an idea person, loyal to a fault, and forgiving. No matter what I've achieved in my life and career, I will never forget where I came from and who helped me along the way. It is partly because of those early mentors that I'm generous with both my time and knowledge, and I'm willing to help wherever I can, whenever I can. But this also goes back to what drives me – a deep belief that this industry, this space, can be the catalyst to change countless people's lives. At the end of the day, it all comes down to belief, in yourself, in others, in this opportunity.

I'd say that one of my most important qualities is that I show up. If I tell somebody that they can count on me and I have their backs, they know that, even if push comes to shove, I will show up for them.

I took a test recently to determine my best strengths. Number 1 was *perspective*. I'd never thought of that as a strength, but I think that is actually true for me. At this point in my career, I do have a unique perspective formed over decades. So, I really do believe that my greatest gift might be perspective, some inherent and some earned.

MY THREE "TELL-ALL" TIPS

1. Some of my best advice is to marry the process and divorce the results. Remember, you're in the choice business. Our job is to go out every day and offer people choices – and continue to offer them choices. You work with the ones who say "Yes," but you don't pass judgement on those who choose "No." It's their choice. To me, that's key. In order to be successful, you can't become emotionally invested in what someone else does. It's up to them. So, you marry the process and the way of doing things. You don't try to modify everything just to make a sale or to handle objections. You simply repeat the proven process over and over again. You divorce yourself from what someone else does or doesn't do.

2. Long-term success is creating wonderful experiences to the best of your ability with the people that are your loyal raving fan customers. Creating a fantastic experience is more than having a great product. It's like Zappos. They sell great shoes, but from the minute you call them, they create an experience that makes you want to keep giving Zappos your business. If you don't create great experiences, then people will think, "I can get shoes anywhere." The person you treat well and tries your product, even one who decides it isn't for him, may recommend you to 10 of his friends based simply on how well he was treated.

3. One of the topics I train on these days is specificity. Most people are not specific enough or don't have a clear enough vision about what they want to create or the goal they want to

achieve. They say they want to make money, but they don't know what they'd do with it. But if you don't know exactly what you want, you'll settle for something that you don't. So very often, even if you achieve the goal, it's like getting to the top of the wrong mountain. So, the more specific you are, the better chance you have of achieving what you really want. Say you want your own home. It has to have three bedrooms, two baths with a living room and a kitchen. We drive up to a house, and you open the door to see its purple walls and green floors and hot pink fixtures. But it has three bedrooms, two baths, a living room and a kitchen. You got what you asked for, but you weren't specific enough on what you really wanted. Does that house match what you said you wanted? Yes, but it's a nightmare of a psychedelic house you're in. Here's the Lisa-ism takeaway: "If you fail to master the art of specificity, you will most definitely master the art of settling."

If you could go back in time when you started your first business in network marketing and you could start all over again, what would you do differently?

Hindsight being what it is, there are a lot of things I'd do differently if I could go back to the beginning. At the end of the day, I would tell my younger self to not worry about what others think. I'd take the business more seriously and myself less seriously. I was always authentic, even at the beginning. I was the mom in ponytails and didn't try to be anything else, even though I felt like more was expected from the industry. I felt back then that being myself was costing me, but I eventually realized that it was a great strength. Don't feel like being you is going to cost you – be unapologetically you! That authenticity is what will help take you to the top, and, ultimately, it did for me.

Here's the bottom line to my career in network marketing and what I know today: The longer I do this, the more I believe; the more I believe, the more people I help; the more people I help, the more I believe. And so it goes.

For three decades, Lisa Grossmann has focused her career primarily on building and nurturing her numerous teams. She has witnessed the power of this industry to create lives enriched beyond imagination. A true believer in network marketing, Lisa's authenticity and willingness to share knowledge has made her highly desired as a mentor, visionary, and thought leader.

11

ANOUK MALAIKA FLAMBERT

I couldn't tell you what I had for dinner last week, or what I did on my last birthday, but I'll never forget the day I was first introduced to my company. I was sitting in a coffee shop in front of a stranger my friend had connected me to. My arms were crossed tightly in front of my chest, and the look on my face said I'm too important for this, so make it quick. But yet, something had gotten me there that day.

When people ask why I got started in network marketing, the story I tell usually centers on how I was looking for a change career-wise. And I was—100%. But there was also a deeper reason I was there, one that was so hard to accept I couldn't even see it myself at the time.

I'd gotten my Bachelor's degree from an Ivy League college, and after graduating with a Master's in Economics, I stumbled into market research and fell head over heels in love with a profession I continued in for 20 years. I climbed the corporate ladder, travelled, got loved on by clients and worked on awesome projects. After having kids, I tried for a few years to pretend that I was one of those cool-as-a-cucumber working moms who could juggle it all.

But the truth was, becoming a mom changed me. So when missing milestones had me crying myself to sleep every night, I quit my job and started offering consulting services from home. It was one of the scariest decisions I'd ever made.

Throughout my childhood, my father's wavering business fortunes had been a major reason for quarrels between my parents, and when, at the age of 23, I lost my dad to suicide, I concluded that entrepreneurship = financial failure = tragedy. There was *no* way I would have gone into private practice if it weren't that my own mental sanity was on the line. But it was. And so I did.

I got lucky at first, as referrals lead to easy business early on. When my income surpassed my previous salary, I started to feel like maybe I *could* do this self-employed thing after all. That is until the proverbial doo hit the fan. In January 2008, the financial market crisis wiped out six months of contract income just as my marriage ended.

I remember sitting in my room after putting the boys to bed, visualizing having to share a 1-bedroom apartment with my two kids and clean toilets to make ends meet. But you know, there's this thing that happens when a woman is up against a wall to provide for her kids. This deep well of strength shows up with what I can only describe as a deafening calm.

And so, *nonetheless, I persisted.* I dialed for dollars, expanded my services to pick up whatever other work I could and, by the end of that year, I had managed to keep my home, piece my income back together and see my two well-balanced sons through their first year post-divorce.

Importantly, that year also gave me my first glimpse of the sense of freedom of choice and control that comes with owning your own business — that knowledge that you can survive on grit and wit no matter what the world throws at you. That was a feeling I never wanted to lose touch with again. So, needless to say, it was deeply disturbing to me to find myself about to throw in the towel just a few years later.

The thing is, once I realized I loved being in business for myself, the necessary next step was to grow my company into one that could finance my bucket list projects and retirement. I tried for a few years, but it turned out to be my Alamo. The fact is, creating a *leveraged* business requires a level of confidence and resilience that I just did not have back then.

Fortunately, during this time, my personal life provided welcome respite as I fell in love, remarried and had my 3rd and 4th sons. But, that honeymoon ended with maternity leave, and as I tried to get my business going again, the dread returned. The internet had made competition tougher, clients were more and more demanding, and my time off for family had highlighted a major drawback of consulting work: when you are trading time for money, you can't reduce your hours without a cut in pay. Ever.

With rising debt and four kids to provide for, *money* became the thing that kept me up at night. My husband and I explored every option: real estate, part-time jobs, even rideshare. But with four kids and two full careers, we did not have enough time or money to spare for any of them to make a real impact.

And so, by the time I put my ego aside enough to go sit in front of that lady in the coffee shop (her name is Paulina Podgorska, by the way, and I will be forever grateful to her for being brave enough to make the ask), the real reason I was there is that I was feeling utterly and completely trapped financially. I had literally started to believe that most of my "one-day" dreams would actually *never* happen, and that thought filled me with despair.

As I listened to her presentation, frankly, I was stunned. I mean, it was EVERYTHING I had been looking for: a path to extra income that I could start on for relatively nothing; a system set-up to be run part-time from wherever and whenever, designed to fit around family and career; 24/7 connection to other entrepreneurs for moral support and motivation, strength and that most magical ingredient of all to anyone who knows anything about business: a time leveraged system for generating residual income. I mean, choirs of angels sang as I sat there. I played my poker face and told her I would have to think about it, but frankly, deep down, she had me at scalable. A 3-way call, and five days later, I jumped in.

My first year moved pretty quickly. I hit the averages and climbed halfway to the top level of my company, a strong start I really needed given how unsure I was that I had what it took to succeed at this. I mean, I had never sold products before, and my consulting business failed *because* I lacked the confidence to prospect. But fear of failure was probably one of my greatest assets at the beginning. That and the fear of looking like a fool.

Once I had told the first few people that I joined a network marketing company, my ego was too big to fail. Instead of the recommended four launches, the first two made me so nauseous I held eight, just to bulldoze through to the other side of fear ASAP. When my upline told me to do something, being notoriously stubborn, I would argue – "there was no way, they were crazy, I couldn't possibly do that" and immediately proceed to do it anyway. I believed in the business model so much more than I did in myself that I started with the goal of hitting an income of $350 per month within 18 months. It was paltry, but it was the amount I was missing to afford the private school I wanted for my son, and it was all I dared to desire. But when my first teeny-weeny 3-person downline helped me surpass that goal in month 3, I caught my first glimpse of the residual income potential this business offered and decided to upsize my dreams.

I had two other experiences that really sealed the deal for me that first year. The first was when the learning curve on my new job forced me to pull back from my business for a few months. That's when I got to experience the value of a supportive upline and a system that functions independently of your presence. The second came a month after I hit my second rank when a corporate restructuring had me sitting in a career re-orientation session with a bunch of other layoff victims whose stress levels and despair were such a palpable contrast to what I was feeling that, that day, I truly grasped the value of hope. It used to sound so hokey to me when I heard network marketers referred to as hope dealers. "Hope" to me signaled pipe-dreams. But the truth is, this business provides people with a context in which they can tap into and unleash the power, skills and the potential to turn their pipe-dreams into reality like no other environment out there. That is, if they want to.

As I write, I have been with my company for six and a half years. I've promoted to new ranks, lost them and gained them back. I've earned trips and incentives, crossed the stage, lost teams and rebuilt new ones several times over. My side-hustle income has helped finance education, travel, braces, renovations and my husband's passion project. I've made the richest new friendships and reconnected with people going back 40 years. But the biggest benefit by far is the woman I have become: Seven years ago, I was imprisoned in a life constrained by fear and self-doubt. Today, I am pulled forward by a future I have created and, and it gives me shivers every time I say this: I, Anouk Malaika Flambert, have become one of the bravest women I know.

I feel like my journey through this profession has been defined by three major lessons that I would like to share with you. The first is one I often share with teammates who struggle with self-confidence, and that is that, contrary to popular belief, confidence is *not* a personality trait but rather the acquisition of competency through practice. We all know the difference between going into an exam in school confident versus underconfident. It simply comes down to how much you studied, practised and prepared. Network marketing is no different. While you should never wait to feel masterful *before* taking action, deciding to choose one tiny skill to study and practice each month will build your competency *and* your confidence. Make it something small and specific, like learning a way to find more people to prospect and putting that technique in action for 15 minutes a day for a month. Or trying on a new response to prospects who go AWOL and following up with all of those for one month. Or picking part of your product or service line-up to master so you can practice upselling benefits and create ten opportunities to do that in one month. It doesn't really matter which ones you pick. What matters most is that making one micro-skill-improvement part of your DMO (Daily Method of Operation) month after month will help you integrate that you *can* master any skill you lack confidence in simply by scheduling-in time for acquiring competence.

The second major lesson has to do with team building. Everyone always said I was a "natural leader". Turns out that what passes for leadership in other areas in life (in my case, charisma and a gift for the verb) has nothing to do with what it takes to be a leader in network marketing. And so, my early failure to create duplication and the number of my teams that evaporated into thin air shook me to my core. I had to learn to focus more on longevity than on production when it comes to leading a team. Because, whatever the business, the real gold is when entrepreneurs stay the course. Creating a team culture akin to a fireplace, where people want to congregate because it makes them feel warm and safe and valued, became my mantra. Especially *safe*. Because most people who join our business need to be given time to have their inner entrepreneur coaxed out of them. And, like a mother, when we see and shine a light on the inner wonder within each person we meet, and offer a judgement-free space in which each individual feels safe to begin to explore the person within that attracted this opportunity in the first place, *that* is when we create *self*-motivated teammates and leaders. As I always say, we are *entrepreneurial incubators*.

Which brings me to lesson three, *Be the Reason*. Every leader in our industry will tell you that their biggest breakthrough came when they started making this business about others and not themselves. What that looks like is described in different ways by each of us, but it is an absolute universal truth. I am always loathe to share that as a prerequisite for success, though because I think most people start their businesses driven by a need or an insecurity that is so strong that asking them to think outside themselves is just not realistic at first. For me, it sometimes had me wondering if I was too selfish or self-absorbed to succeed. For every little moment in your life, when you were faced with an obstacle that you chose to overcome, there is someone out there waiting to hear just that story, who sees themselves in you just enough to give them the courage to take another step forward, to rise above a limitation or perhaps even to not give up. This industry is about understanding that *you are the reason* for someone.

Most of us cannot remember what we had for dinner last week or what we did on our last birthday, but we remember the day we first said yes to network marketing. Because choosing this is one of those moments in life when we were guided by something greater than us. So know that if you were guided to this industry, you were *called* to *be the reason for someone.* And on days when you don't think you are worthy enough to do it for you, do it for them.

If you could go back in time when you started your first business in network marketing and you could start all over again, what would you do differently?

If I had to pick *one* thing, it would definitely be to *follow the fun!* It's a line my team hears me use often, starting with the first strategy call with a new partner. Most of us are doing this business part-time alongside all kinds of other commitments (work, family and plenty else) that are usually way more important and will probably remain so until your network marketing income grows big enough to make an impact. Which means that for most of us, that might take a while.

And on top of that, for most of us, doing the work of this business leaves us feeling pretty inadequate and incapable when we first get started. It's no wonder income-producing activity quickly becomes the last thing you feel motivated to do and the first thing to take a back seat to your other commitments. So, unless (or until) you are one of those rare birds who really believes you have it in you to turn this business into a boon fast, *follow the fun.* On a monthly or weekly or even daily basis, figure out which part of "doing this business" feels the most fun to you, and start with that. Include a little fun in your DMO every day. If it's the personal development audios, eat those for breakfast. Fancy yourself a future speaker, go live on social and let your upline know you are juiced by opportunities to share. Love playing with products or organizing events, build it in. Find a part of this business that is as enjoyable to you as your favorite retail therapy session or a foot massage, and you'll fit it. "Eat that frog" works when the benefits are immediate. Until then, *follow the fun.*

Anouk Malaika Flambert is an economist and self-described international nomad. Born to a Haitian father and Sri Lankan mother, she grew up in both countries until moving to the US for university. Today, she lives in Montreal with her husband and four sons.

12

CINDY HAFENBRACK

Fall in Love with Your Journey

Yup, I just wanted a new bedspread.

This was the dream that propelled me to jump into this industry.

We need to go back 27 years ago when my love for this extraordinary industry of Network Marketing began.

I was sitting at the little gym with my two young sons, Andy, age seven and Matt age four, and this gal kept smiling at me. I thought to myself, do I know her? We started chatting, and she told me she just started a home-based business with a children's book publisher and asked if I wanted to take a look at her catalog. Of course, I said yes.

Then she nonchalantly mentioned that her friend who told her about this company was earning a great monthly income from her home. I thought to myself, no way. I mean, I had heard of people making money in home-based businesses, but never anyone I knew or anyone local.

Then my wheels started turning, and I thought to myself, "Hey, maybe I could make a little money and buy that $200 bedspread I had my eye on." It was an expensive bedspread, that's why I had to jump into Network Marketing!

I definitely caught the vision of this industry right away. I got so excited about the possibilities and started to imagine what the future could be like if I got serious and kept my eye on the prize.

I kept saying to myself if that woman can make that income every month, so can I.

This is definitely a mindset that has benefited me throughout my network marketing career.

In fact, when I think of what has benefitted me the most on my journey, it has been mindset, perseverance and gratitude.

If I saw someone else succeeding, I felt I could too. I always felt they don't have anything I don't have. I never said the words, "I can't. "

I wanted what I saw other people achieving in this industry. I wanted the time freedom and the financial rewards. Yes, I fell in love with this industry. When I first discovered this industry, I was shocked that something this wonderful existed. Being able to create a beautiful dream life for my family and help others do the same, well, it just didn't get any better than this.

I rolled up my sleeves, put on my blinders, and I decided I would do something every day in my business to help bring me one step closer to my goals. I can't remember another time in my life when I was this consistent. However, I was so excited about what this industry could do for my life and the lives of others, I simply just set out to go for it and change some lives.

I fell in love with the journey. I fell in love with taking people from not knowing to knowing about my opportunity. I was so elated with what I had in my hot hands I couldn't wait to tell people about it. I had the ability to make a huge difference and impact on other people's lives. Not everyone has the opportunity to accomplish this, but in this industry, we do.

Fall in love with your why. Otherwise known as keeping your eye on the prize. I joined this industry to give my two boys a better life. This industry gave me hope for a better future and the license to dream again.

As a single mom, I wanted to show my two boys I could do anything I set my mind to. I wanted them to be proud of me. I wanted them to see their mom could make a decision, execute it and stay the course.

To help keep me on track and stay motivated, I made a list of twenty dreams and by twenty dreams, I mean twenty things I wanted this industry to pay for. The dreams started out as survival dreams like pay off my credit card and pay off my dentist. My first dream on the list was to buy organic food. With all the dreams I could possibly come up with, that was my first dream. I had to laugh. Then the dreams got to be more fun as you went down the list, take the boys to New York for Christmas to see their grandmother, buy my mom a new car, buy my son a new car, go visit my son Andy at College in Singapore, take the whole family to Italy and Spain. I read this list every day. Plus, I taped it to the wall. I also had my two sons tape pictures of their dreams up on the wall. I knew I would work harder on their dreams. I also taped 8 by 10 pictures of their smiling faces up on the wall overlooking my phone and computer.

On days I didn't feel like working, I just looked up at their faces and said to myself, Cindy, keep going, you're doing this for them. Plus, I heard someone say once, it's good to build a financial wall that can protect your family from impact. Believe me, impact is going to happen. You never know when, but trust me, it will happen.

I never wanted to look at my two sons in the eyes and say to them, remember that great business mommy started, and I told you what a great life it was going to give us? Well, I quit.

Nothing was going to stop me from giving my boys a better life and the life of our dreams.

Was I scared, tired and overwhelmed at times? Yes! But I heard acting in spite of fear was courage. I said to myself, Cindy, you need to get a grip and have courage (I do a ton of self-talk).

People told me this *wouldn't work,* and *don't do it.* However, that just fueled my fire.

A few years ago, my son Matt said to my mom, "Grandma, are you proud of my mom?" My mom said, "*Yes, I am Matt.*" Matt said, "*Yes, Grandma, I am too.*" What more could I want?

Fall in love with what this industry can do for your life and live your life in gratitude. I have been very blessed in this industry. I wake up every morning with gratitude and joy because of the kind of life this industry has given to me and my family. My mission is to help others achieve what they want and also have a better life.

When I first discovered this industry, I said to myself, Cindy, this is the kind of business you have waited your whole life for. This is going to change your life, your children's life, your mother's life and anyone else who wants to lock arms with me, and together we can help each other go after our dreams. I have so much gratitude for what this industry has done for my life, and I know what it can do for others.

In fact, I felt negligent if I didn't tell them about it. And what is the girlfriend code of honor? When you find something you love, you tell them about it. Right!?

I am extremely grateful that this industry has given me the time freedom to be with my family when they need me. When my 90-year-old mother needs me, I can drop everything and hop on the next plane to help her. When my son needs me to babysit my four-year-old grandson for a few days a week, I am available! You can't put a price on time freedom.

To sum it all up, here are my tips:

- Fall in love with your journey
- Fall in love with contacting people to enlighten them about your opportunity
- Fall in love with your list of 20 dreams
- Fall in love with your future
- Fall in love with changing lives

It just so happens that network marketing turns out to be a dream career that is just waiting for you to serve you on a silver platter anything you desire in life! Dream big. Dream your wildest dreams. You know about network marketing now.

If you could go back in time when you started your first business in network marketing and you could start all over again, what would you do differently?

If I could go back and do something different, it would be to jump in to personal development sooner. I would have started my journey of reading personal development books much sooner. In the beginning, the only thing I had in the way of personal development was a tape titled *"Feel the Fear and Do it Anyway."* I listened to that tape (dating myself here) over and over and over again.

Cindy has been a Network Marketing Professional since 1994. Prior to this industry, Cindy was a registered nurse. Helping people has always been her passion, and Cindy found her calling in Network Marketing. Cindy has a huge heart for helping others see the possibilities and go after their dreams. She feels Network Marketing is one of the best vehicles out there to help people accomplish whatever they desire and to have a beautiful life.

13

TRACY ANDERSON

Twenty years ago, I thought my life was nearly perfect. I was married, had three precious children, and had just built my dream home. I worked from home running my husband's medical practice and was able to be home with my kids while still contributing to the household. It was everything I had ever wanted.

Without warning, my life turned upside down, and I abruptly found myself divorced, broke, unemployed and desperate to find a way to support myself and my three young children. Finding a way to work from home was essential as I didn't want to miss a minute of my kid's lives as they grew up. I wanted to go to all their soccer games, their school field trips and band concerts. I wanted to be there when they came home from school and when they stayed home sick. One thing was clear... I needed to be my own boss.

My solution at the time came in the form of a traditional business designing kitchens and selling cabinets. While it was time-consuming work, it served its purpose as I could set my own hours and earn the income I needed. Unfortunately, this business came to an end following the housing market crash of 2008. After a couple years of struggling to stay afloat, the business went under and once again, I found myself in the difficult position of having no income and a family to support. To make matters worse, I was also deep in business debt, my credit was shot, my house was on the verge of foreclosure, and my car was repossessed right out of my driveway. Life was stressful, to say the least, and while I thought that I had hit rock bottom, it turned out I still had further to fall.

About this time, a friend invited me to a business presentation where I learned that I could start my own business in the Network Marketing industry with a very small initial investment. I loved that it was turn-key and that once enrolled, I would have my own website, and I would be instantly open for business. I was attracted to the concept of leveraged, residual income, having no overhead and the ability to get into profit mode right away. I was intrigued by the business model. I left that meeting with a copy of the compensation plan and the intention of thinking it over for a few days. I had hope.

That decision time accelerated when the very next morning, I was running errands, and my debit card declined. Now, this wasn't the first time that happened, but I knew that my child support check had just been deposited and was baffled. I sat in my car and pulled up my bank account online only to discover that the Department of Revenue had attached my bank account for past unpaid taxes on my failed cabinet business. They helped themselves to my child support, leaving my account balance at $0. But that wasn't even the worst part – they also drained all three of my kid's savings accounts. I had never felt so vulnerable and powerless in all my life. This was when I realized what rock bottom really felt like. I was in total despair, and I put my head in my hands and cried. Then the magic happened, as at this moment I noticed something on the floor of my car. The compensation plan that I had picked up at the meeting the night before was right at my feet. This was my clue. I knew without a doubt that the answer I was seeking was right in front of me.

That very day, I took a leap of faith and jumped into this industry and never looked back! I didn't just dip a toe in to test the Network Marketing waters. I jumped in with both feet because failure was not an option for me.

I was committed, coachable and driven, and I rapidly grew a team of other like-minded people who were also searching for answers. Looking back now, I can see that all roads led me to where I am today, and I don't regret a single moment of my journey. I found a home in this industry. More than that, I found a community of people that love and support me, I found the income stream I needed, and I found solutions.

Because of this industry, I was able to pull my house out of foreclosure, pay down debt (past business taxes included!), support my family, and continue to be my own boss and live life on my terms. This year I bought my dream home in Arizona. I will forever have the power to design the life of my choosing because of that leap of faith.

Because of this industry, I have peace of mind in knowing when my mortgage payment comes due, I can send off a payment that very day. I have the freedom to come and go as I please, to travel, and to wake up without an alarm. But most important to me, I have the security in knowing that I always have a safety net for myself and my kids.

The most gratifying part of being in this industry is empowering others to take control of their life. By helping people to build their own businesses, they are able to pay off debt, buy their dream home, put their kids in costly sports camps, start college funds, and quit jobs to be at home with their kids, fill their grocery carts and gas tanks, and simply start to dream again. The rewards of seeing others succeed are tremendous.

Trust your journey. Life leaves clues. You are meant to be exactly where you are right now, and you are meant to be reading this book. I believe that you, too, can design the life of your choosing. Whether you need $100 a month or much more, Network Marketing is a vehicle for you to take charge of your life.

3 Tell All Tips:

1. Show up every day. If you want to be your own boss, make sure you are an effective boss. If you want to schedule your own hours, be sure to put your business on the schedule. If you don't show up, you won't succeed. Consistency is key. Whether you have 5 minutes to dedicate or 5 hours, commit to working your business on some level every day.

2. Be a good listener. When talking to people about what you have to offer, learn to ask good questions and then listen to their answers. In this way, you will discover what their needs are and have solutions to offer. Be genuine. When you approach your business with the pure intention of helping others, people notice. Help them to figure out if what you have – product or opportunity – is a fit for them. In this way, you can feel good about what you do, and people will want to

know about what you have to help them. I am a firm believer that if you do the right thing, the right thing happens.

3. Set the right expectation. It is okay to dream, and I encourage you to dream big! But it is imperative that you set reasonable, attainable goals based on how much time and energy you have to put into your business. We want you to feel empowered and not discouraged! We all come into this industry with different time constraints, backgrounds, networks, and skills. Therefore, we all grow our businesses at a different speed. To have success, we have to grow in three critical areas: our skill set, our network and, last but not least, we have to grow ourselves. Give yourself the time and the grace to grow in these ways while always remembering why you are here.

If you could go back in time when you started your first business in network marketing and you could start all over again, what would you do differently?

I wouldn't change a thing. Each step in my Network Marketing journey has been essential to having success and getting to where I am now. I am not with the same company I started with, but I ended up exactly where I needed to be. I am also not the same person I was when I started and have become a better version of myself! Looking back, I can say that personal growth has been just as life-changing as financial growth. The lesson here is to fully commit to the journey and embrace every high and low. Strap yourself in and enjoy the ride as there is nothing else out there that can take you somewhere so truly spectacular!

Tracy Anderson has been an entrepreneur her entire adult life. Having developed a passion for health and wellness at an early age, her business and nutrition interests happily converged in the network marketing industry.

Tracy is passionate about protecting the earth and all the creatures that inhabit it. Empowering others to enjoy a better quality of life through health, wealth, and freedom is her greatest reward.

14

SARA WEISS

My name is (SassBoss) Sara Weiss from Ottawa, Canada, and I joined the Network Marketing industry when I was 21 (12 years ago).

I definitely didn't have a childhood I can brag about. Before getting into Network Marketing, I grew up in a low-income family without a father and my three younger sisters. My mother had me when she was only 18 years old and had a terrible taste in abusive men. I had the challenge of spending 11 years growing up with a man who verbally abused us all daily and sometimes physically. Experiencing all of this and my mom attempting to leave him, yet always going back with the reason being that she couldn't afford to take care of us on her own, I felt weak and helpless for my family. I felt like we were doomed and trapped… I realized that I NEVER wanted to be weak, dependent on a man's money or unable to give my family a life of freedom and joy. I realized I had to find a way to create my own wealth instead of building it for others or having no control over my family's well-being!

I obviously didn't grow up with incredible role models for creating wealth or doing business and sales or marketing, nor did I have anything other than what I considered limitations and disadvantages. Living with the idea that I was at a disadvantage was a dangerous limiting belief that would only keep me right where I was, thinking I was doomed to repeat my mother's life, and it took me getting involved in Network Marketing to start a long journey of personal development to figure that out.

I began reading books like *How to Win Friends and Influence People, Think and Grow Rich, Rich Dad Poor Dad* and *The 21 Irrefutable Laws Of Leadership,* and my mind began to shift. Not only did my mindset improve, but I began to fall in love with the personal development behind network marketing! I was so happy on the exciting rollercoaster of Network Marketing and learning how to recruit even though I was sucked horribly at it. I was 21 years old trying to recruit others my age for a home services Network Marketing and was able to build a bit of a team, but they didn't have money to spend or homes for home services, haha. I ended up spending days at the shopping mall trying to meet new people so I could share this amazing opportunity, and low and behold, I met a few people that joined my network and some even joined my team, yet I continued to make little to no money! All I knew for sure was that I kept growing and learning with every new book and every failure.

Early on, something that stuck with me was that if I wanted to truly succeed in network marketing or any field for that matter, I would need to become a professional. When you think of what being a professional means, you probably think of someone who's polished and paid very well for being a master of their craft, and that's what I imagined. Think of professional sports athletes or professional businessmen and women. What do you think it took for them to get where they are? I knew it wouldn't happen overnight. Professionals take all the courses, they read all the books, they fail and make mistakes over and over. They stay the course and don't give up until they are a professional, and even once they are professionals, they continue to grow and learn how to be an even more effective professional in their field.

I embraced this process, and I went through exactly what I shared. I see many people get into Network Marketing and win big in their first year, but that was not the case for me. It took me five years, and four or five different Network Marketing companies before I made a paycheck that was worth considering with a health shake company. I celebrated my years of consistency and dedication to growth by going on vacation to Cancun. It was during this phase of my network marketing experience that I began to understand it better. I began to understand what was important when it came to recruiting and getting customers. I realized how important it was to build relationships for the sake of building relationships and not for the sake of looking for a yes or no to join my team or buy my products. I teach network marketers to stop going for no or going for yes and to spend their time becoming professional relationship builders. When you pressure yourself to get a yes or no from your prospect, you pass that pressure on to them, and in most cases, it only pushes people away from you or shows them that you don't truly care about them.

Our connections and relationships with others lead to incredible miracles; from love, to dream careers, opportunities, and other things, connections with others can drastically improve the quality of your life. Think about this for a second... if you spent your life just creating friendships and connections with a goal of 1 million friends, all of which you had built a real connection with, how fast could you accomplish anything? If you became broke and destitute and asked your 1 million friends for a dollar, you'd be a millionaire! If you had a choice between 1 million dollars or 1 million friends, what would you choose? Do you, like me, see that 1 million friends are worth much, much more than 1 million dollars? Knowing that, do you also see how building genuine relationships with people is much more valuable than "going for a yes or no?"

That all being said, while you are prospecting, I wouldn't AVOID inviting someone to see your information. I would just be much more interested in them and creating a relationship with them – which if you do, chances are it will come up in conversation naturally, or if it doesn't right away, it will come up later when the timing is better. All I'm saying is that when I shifted to becoming a professional relationship builder, my network expanded along with my success in more areas than just network marketing!

When reading this book, you might be thinking that you will finally have the recipe and strategies to follow for success! What if I told you that success is only 20% strategy and 80% psychology? Want to know how a college dropout with an abusive childhood, a drug addict father that wasn't present and an odd person like me is now creating wealth after being on welfare only three years ago?

I stopped defining myself by my past and present situation. I stopped thinking of myself as disadvantaged and started to define myself by who I wanted to become! I created a vision of not only the life I wanted but who I was in that life, even if I had no idea how it would happen. I saw myself as a powerhouse businesswoman, well dressed, confident, amazing posture, high self-esteem and a presence that empowered others as soon as they heard me speak! I saw my life change as I became clearer and clearer on my purpose in life and how I wanted to live it. I soon realized that my vision created a belief that in turn made me extremely passionate about my life, and that led to endless energy! I am constantly high energy now, and as you probably know, energy is the source of all creation in our lives. We take that energy, and we CREATE!

If you are operating without a clear vision of who you are becoming and your purpose in life, then you will be hard-pressed to believe in anything, including yourself – which will prevent you from feeling that incredible passion I speak about or the energy that comes with it. It all starts with your vision! When you operate with vision, belief, passion and energy, then you will always find a way to be successful, and you will light people up when you connect with them!

Would you like a piece of very high-value coaching? My Tell-All! To accomplish anything:

- You must first know WHY you want to accomplish it.

- You must make a DECISION to accomplish it.

- You must know what SUPPORT you need to accomplish it.

- You must prepare your response to the things that will try and DERAIL YOU from accomplishing it.

- You must take ONE STEP towards accomplishing it.

- And you MUST REPEAT this every day to accomplish it!

This is the formula for success. The problem with it is that the single most important trait of anyone who is successful in network marketing or anything else is also the hardest for most people to do and the reason so many give up. Consistency. Too many people give up too soon before they can ever become a professional and benefit from the fruit of their labour. I gave you a powerful strategy, but if you don't use the psychology I shared with you, that strategy will not work for you.

When you are in the relationship-building business, you will quickly realize that people don't care what you have to sell; they only care about themselves! If you want to influence people for anything in life, the only way to do it is to give people what they want, and the only way to do that is to find out what they want. If you start blasting off at people about what you like about the product or service you are offering based on what YOU want, you are rarely going to appeal to the person you are prospecting. The best way to find out what people want can be as simple as asking what they want, but sometimes it can take a bit more work. Ask questions that give your friend an opportunity to talk about themselves. Asking good questions is a skill that can be improved, and if you learn to ask good questions, you will begin to get good answers and all the information you need to not only figure out what they want but to also build a stronger relationship and connection with that person!

If you market a weight loss product and you start a conversation with someone and have a genuine conversation with interest in THEM, you might ask questions about who they are, what they are up to and their interests. Chances are if you ask the right questions, they might tell you about their health and maybe even about putting on extra weight during the pandemic or winter; then you can ask questions based on what they plan to do about it or what their goals are. The more you dig deeper on the who, what, where, when, why and how, the more you will know how to help them with what you have, and you can then offer them information on a solution that could help. Just make sure you're not grilling them with questions like it's an interrogation. Show genuine interest and have a very authentic conversation. If you love and are passionate about what you do, then you should be able to have a fun conversation that leads to you getting to know them better and building a stronger connection at the same time as finding out what they want and providing a possible solution.

Everybody is capable of greatness with a great vision and belief, which if you model other successful people, you will see that they all have incredible vision and belief. Do what they do, and you will have similar results. Be true to who you are, not a robot and as I always say, "Embrace your Sass and chase your dreams because they're not going to chase you!"

If you could go back in time when you started your first business in network marketing and you could start all over again, what would you do differently?

If I could go back in time and start my career in network marketing all over again, to ensure faster success, I would tell myself to focus more on what unconditional value I can spread across social media in all forms of content. I would assure myself that I will become massively successful and to operate with that confidence and posture instead of desperation. I would also tell myself to not talk so much and focus more on listening by asking better questions!!!

———

#1 Best-Selling Leadership Education Author, High-Performance Success Coach, International Motivational Speaker and a Top Leader in the Network Marketing industry.

Sara has been abused, lied to and cheated on, and it's cost her friends and family. She's been fired from jobs she loved, has been on welfare and is a single mom. She has been ridiculed for being different and endured hatred as the label "transgender" has been forced upon her. She experienced a lonely existence as she was buried deep in victim mentality.

She found the strength to rise above, creating a level of self-confidence she never imagined she could have. She's overcome her challenging experiences to create an enriched life that she has always dreamed of. She is now a leader, a coach and an inspiration for people to live their greatest lives. She has become a source of motivation to help people achieve the highest version of themselves. Looking at all of her accomplishments, it's clear she was not born this way and taking control of her life made all the difference. Her book *(Not) Born This Way* not only reveals the paths she took but might be the guiding light you need to empower you to redefine your story and create your greatest life ever inside and outside of Network Marketing!

15

DANA NICHOLSON

Twenty years ago, I was alone while my husband, Neil, was away on military deployment, I didn't have a whole lot of belief in myself. I was heartbroken at the thought of leaving my six-month-old daughter to return to work full-time to keep up with the bills we had at the time. When I opened my first jar of salsa mix all those years ago, I really had no idea of the opportunity that lay ahead and would lead me on the journey to be one of the highest-paid women in my company in North America. Even as I write these words, I cannot believe it some days. I've been thinking a lot about how things have changed, and when you drill down, it really hasn't:

My company 2000 versus My company 2020

Same amazing products. Same Opportunity. Same three Requirements, which are also my tips to you:

1. A Dream.
2. A Work Ethic.
3. A Positive Belief in yourself and in my company

A Dream

I've always been a dreamer, that's come naturally to me. I remember as a child, I would daydream and sometimes be scolded for it. What I didn't realize back then is how it would serve me throughout my life and especially my chosen career in direct sales. Once I started my business, I was encouraged to read, and one of the most impactful books I read was *The Magic of Thinking Big* by David J. Schwartz, Ph.D. Today there is so much more understanding about how we can train our brain and access to education through the internet and podcasts. Without a doubt, being a dream gave me an edge in my business.

A Work Ethic

A strong work ethic was part of my upbringing as my parents and extended family came from a long line of people who knew how to work. As a teen and into adulthood, I often had multiple jobs because I was taught if you want something, you have to go out and earn the money. I took pride in learning and mastering new skills in all of the jobs that I had leading up to my career in direct sales. I waitressed, was a legal assistant and worked in human resources.

A Positive Belief in Myself

The biggest obstacle to me in starting my business 20 years ago was a belief in myself. You see, I had to learn to overcome the fact that the fear of rejection and failure is an ever-present voice that I wrestled with. We have all that voice in our head, which is linked directly to self-confidence and our ability to believe in ourselves. My voice was loud back then, and I had a tendency to second guess myself. Do you hear that same voice? I am here to tell you that through personal growth, I have learned to keep that voice subdued, which has allowed me to lead and grow a business beyond my wildest dreams.

Ups-and-downs are a natural part of a career. The first was learning to believe in myself and my ability. The second has been having to rebuild my business in several different cities as we moved for Neil's military career. In the early days, we moved around a few times, and I really had to put myself out there in each new city we arrived in. That fear of rejection would come up from time-to-time, and I really had to push myself to reach out to new people and to build a network and so, I've learned to work my business with confidence and to accept that no is an answer and it actually means maybe and become a stronger and more effective entrepreneur. I also have committed to attending every company event because there is so much value in being with people who "get it." Even after 20 years, being around like-minded people motivates me more-and-more each time.

Massive action is a requirement to build any business. Learning to work consistently and pace up over the years is how my business thrived. My husband has always been supportive, and together, we've made the decision for me to work because it has helped us to live a life of design for our family, which now includes four awesome kids and a dream home and property! The opportunity that we have in network marketing is so epic because there isn't a limited number of top positions or ranks that can promote—we are all here to achieve and succeed and make a difference. We are here, and in our hometowns, hustling with heart. And, this opportunity is forgiving, which was so important to me in those early days and over the years. I've made mistakes, I've taken responsibility, I've learned, I've apologized, and it's all a part of my journey.

I am still learning and growing every day, after all these years! As an entrepreneur, I've learned to train and condition myself to plan and hit targets, to create healthy success habits and make the most of the 24 hours I have every day. I've also learned many times over that disorganization is a slow and very painful way to operate. Things become very frustrating when I try to keep them in my head, and I now understand the power in making a "to do" list and freeing my brain of that space to focus on other aspects of my business.

I have also come to understand what a responsibility it is to be of service to others. I know that with my business, I give people confidence in the kitchen to feed their families well. Plus, through the class environment, I give the host and their guests an incredibly fun experience, and this is so important for so many people. Thinking back on myself as a naïve, young mother, I empathize with those who are missing a community connection. When we were posted and moved multiple times, my business really kept me sane and anchored me in a new community. When my husband was deployed, I had my four young kids to focus on, and my business gave me a sense of purpose, and my kids were my reason for working.

I'm often asked about the "cost" to my family and the sacrifices we made by me working from home. I believe that no matter what career you choose or if you don't choose to work, there are sacrifices for the family. Together with my husband, we made this decision based on what was best for our family. Looking back now, I can really see how working my business helped me with my mental health, especially when my husband was deployed. It gave me a sense of purpose beyond my children, which also gave me a connection to an incredible community. My best friends are women I met through my company. I know the power of being in the presence of people and feeding off that mutual energy of growing a business and making a difference. This connection has not only built my confidence, but it has made me a better mother and wife. And I've seen so many examples of how network marketing has helped other people and their families gain confidence and live better lives.

I've learned so much in my 20 years and really believe that my husband and I have created a life of design through my business. We have choices and freedom that I never knew existed because that wasn't modelled to me growing up. My parents had regular 9 to 5 jobs and stayed with their company for 30 years, and they were feeding off a mutual unhappiness. Life doesn't have to be like that! Entrepreneurship for me is freedom, choice and fun, and that's what I've chosen.

So if you have a passion for your company and you wouldn't be reading this if you didn't, dream big, pour your heart into your business because beyond your limitations and insecurities lies the epic life that you deserve.

If you could go back in time when you started your first business in network marketing and you could start all over again, what would you do differently?

The only thing I would do differently is focus more on increasing the belief I had in myself. I was a 10 out of 10 with my belief in my company, and when I realized what held me back was my own mindset, it was powerful. I then spent time ensuring I trained my brain and also challenged the "stories" that I told myself. I spent time ensuring that I put positive and empowering messages, and the best thing I did was that I surrounded myself with people who had a similar or bigger vision and goals. Always check your mindset

Dana Nicholson started her business in the spring of 2000. She is a DSWA Coach Excellence Certified Coach, a Certified DSWA Elite Leader and was very proud to be nominated and win the 2017 Upper Ottawa Valley Chamber of Commerce Entrepreneur of the Year Award. She has also been awarded numerous accolades from her company.

Since her journey into entrepreneurship, Dana has helped thousands of consultants start their business, and she has been a Top Earner. Dana's husband Neil retired from his 23-year military career at the age of 41, and they are the proud parents to three teens and a 21-year-old. They reside in the Ottawa Valley.

16

AMY M. GRASSO

Being an entrepreneur had never been on my radar. I was always told that you graduate high school, and then you go to college, and then you get a 9-5 job working for someone else. Working for ME never crossed my mind. Yet here we are, almost a decade in and one of the best career decisions of my life.

Let's rewind to April of 2011. I had just given birth to my first son, and while I was SO blessed and grateful to become a mama, I had an unhealthy relationship with food and physical activity, a negative mindset. I was overall unhappy, and I had felt lost. Until one day, my husband brought home a burned DVD of a workout program that he suggested we do together. At the time, I was like ... "Um NO.", but he convinced me to give it a go with him.

And I did.
And it changed my life.

It all started there — with a 63-day workout program that helped me to find myself again. It allowed me to push my limits and REALLY opened up the doors to becoming who I was meant to be. I know, sounds cliché, right? But it's true. And to be honest, I talked about this fitness program to anyone and everyone that would listen. Because while yes, I lost some weight… it was more than that. It was a mental shift. And sharing that experience with other mamas like myself, mamas that were in the place where I was, well, it made me feel ALIVE.

About a year had passed, and I was working full time with an 11-month-old baby. I loved my job; I REALLY did. But what I didn't love was leaving my son all day. And I can remember sitting at my desk, on one of those long workdays where I was hit with a major workload and thinking to myself, "Is this what I am meant to do for the rest of my life? Is this REALLY it for me?"

And then this crazy thought came into my head, what if I could spend the rest of my life doing what I loved? And WHAT did I love? Well, besides my family, I had grown to love fitness. I had grown to love inspiring other people to improve their wellness. BOOM. THAT was it, and little did I know … that fitness program that I would SHOUT from the rooftops, I could get PAID through connecting people to it. I could earn an income by using MY experience to improve the lives of others.

And so my Network Marketing journey began.

My journey started slow. I was not one of those people who hit the ground running with their business. I believe that I sat idle, with the business opportunity in the back of my mind for about nine months before I actually started to take action. I would connect people with the program that I loved here and there, but never on a consistent basis. It wasn't until the Holiday season of 2012 that I decided to go all-in simply because I wanted to pay for my son's Christmas in cash.

So I did. I leaned into my upline Mentor, I made a plan, I put the PEOPLE I was serving at the front of my mind, and I went to work. That December, I hit a business goal that is now a non-negotiable. It was to help AT LEAST 5 people with the wellness solution that helped me. And since that month, December 2012... I have not missed a single month of connecting five people with a solution that could work for them.

Those people experienced the same changes and transformations that I did. They then became ADVOCATES for the programs and supplements. They then wanted to do what I was doing. They wanted to get into the business side of things as well because of their BELIEF in what we offered.

Over the years, it grew. The more people I helped, the more people I taught how to make this a business, the more my income grew... but more significant, the more of an impact I made.

But don't get me wrong, there were challenges and obstacles in my journey. It didn't all just fall into place. First, the fear of being "sales-y." However, I got over that fear pretty quick. I was able to allow myself to see that what I was providing to people could make a huge difference in their lifestyles. And why would someone NOT pay for what I had? My BELIEF in what I could provide was way stronger than my fear of being sales-y, and through my conversations with prospects, that confidence showed.

And then, of course, there are the naysayers, those closest to you who make fun of you or don't support you. All of the people who think Network Marketing as a profession is bad, annoying, a nuisance. Overcoming those people, those accusations and allowing them to see that it's not Network Marketing that is bad (it's more closely tied to network market ERS which a bad approach), but something impactful that has been hard. But for me, I have always led my business with heart, integrity, and value.

I always say that we do Network Marketing differently, that we have a unique way of doing this business that makes people feel good. I am a BIG fan of providing people with knowledge, tips and tricks, overall VALUE that they can implement into their daily lives. I want someone to go to my Facebook or Instagram to SEEK out recipes, or workouts, or toddler tips. I want to be more than just a billboard for my company. I want to be my own brand.

I have been given this platform of network marketing to spread light and positivity. I have been given it as a place to serve others, yes, through my company… but SO much more.

I keep it real.
I keep it authentic.
And in a world of perfection, I want people to see that I am perfectly imperfect.
I want them to relate to me on that level, to get to know me, like me, trust me… and then allow me into their lives with some tools built for life change.

Entrepreneurship is challenging. But for those who have an intense belief in themselves and what they can offer, the sky really is the limit. You have to understand that BELIEF is the gateway to success in this type of business. I feel like it took me nine months to get started because I didn't fully understand the POWER that I held within myself. I looked at other people and thought, "That can't be me; I can't reach that level of success." I was standing in my own way, building my own wall. But when I tore that wall to the ground through a LOT of personal development, my business changed. I refused to let NOTHING stand in the way of the life I wanted to create.

In addition, I started to REALLY make my business less about me and more about my people. I talk a lot about adding value, and again, I feel as though this is crucial to building a successful business. People are selfish; they just are! They want to know what is in it for them. How can what YOU DO, or what YOU provide help make their lives better? You post a sweaty selfie after your workout, yay! However, how is that helping someone else? How is that post going to help THEM to get into a workout routine? Tell them! Share the little tidbits of wisdom that help you get through a tough workout. Give them tips on how THEY can be better in this area. Share, give, provide… and then do it some more.

Lastly, in order to be great in this business, you must learn to NOT attach your value or worth to the successes or failures of those on your team. This was a hard lesson to learn for myself, and something that I wish would have been spoken into me early on. I want to see people win, and I want to see them be great, but I know that's on them. I can be there as their cheerleader, their mentor, their upline, but at the end of the day, they need to do the work. If I am showing up, providing resources and leading by example, I am doing my job. I am giving them what they need, but I am not their boss, nor can I do the work for them.

If you could go back in time when you started your first business in network marketing and you could start all over again, what would you do differently?

If I could go back in time and do anything differently with my network marketing business, I would have hit the ground RUNNING when I first enrolled. As mentioned, I sat for nine months doing nothing, and I could have used those nine months to help and serve more people. Other than that, I don't believe that I would want to change anything else. I feel as though all of the obstacles, the failures, the choices and decisions... all of those things created the business that I have today, created the person that I am today. So looking back, while it has been a roller coaster of a ride, there's not much I would change.

Amy Grasso is the mother of two boys, Cameron and Carter, and has been married for over 11 years to her husband, Steve. She was born and raised in Ohio and still resides there with her family. She is super passionate about women's wellness, raising healthy families, and overall inspiring people to improve their lives and reach their goals. For the past nine years, she has been able to use her platform with Network Marketing to tap into her true potential as a motivator and live out a life as an entrepreneur on her own terms! She loves sports, hanging out with her family and getting outdoors.

17

LISA DEMAYO

I Chose Triumphant

"Why don't you go home and be a real mom?"

I stood at the end of a neighbor's driveway, undecided for all of 3 seconds if I should feel defeated or triumphant.

Defeated or triumphant that my "pitch" to take a neighborhood mom along on the journey of network marketing with me was rejected.

Defeated or triumphant that someone wasn't open to what was possible.

Defeated or triumphant with the realization I had to have 1000s of conversations to achieve what I wanted.

I chose triumphant.

Somehow I knew in that moment – that grit, hard work, and all my years focusing on personal development were going to come together. They just had to.

This Is Not A Dress Rehearsal

I was 19 years old when one of my mom's friends invited her to an opportunity meeting. My dad had just died, and my mom was working three jobs. Experiencing death early taught me "this is not a dress rehearsal," and I was going to make the time for my mom, all while changing my plans to move away for college so I could be closer to home.

I was a freshman in college and working full time when she got the call. Despite my crazy schedule, I said, "I'll go with you." I went to support my mom and became fascinated, not so much with the product or the business, but with the people in front of the room.

This was in the early 80s, and from there, I started signing myself up for different coaching courses – anything I came across. Having experienced many adversities during my teenage years, I had become interested in personal coaching at the age of 16. Today I'm trained in many different modalities, including neuro-linguistic programming, somatic coaching, and ontological coaching.

I'm a Master Coach who trains coaches in how to lead leadership groups. I've trained in financial institutions, group settings, and one on one. Along the way, I kept meeting network marketers because they often frequent personal development courses. Many would invite me to their company events. I would watch the behavior of the presenters in front of the room, and I would talk to people.

Young and naïve, I said yes to everyone who invited me. I can't even tell you how many different company conventions I have attended. I wanted to understand how the leaders spoke to their groups, what leadership skills they had. While everybody was taking notes on the product and business statistics, I was observing, "This is where they ask the audience a question," or "This is how the speaker edifies himself." I would then bring what I learned to my coaching business, always a student and a teacher all at once.

I Said "Yes"

I finally, and officially, joined network marketing in 2005, tired of the "rat race." A quick stop after an exhausting road trip – *a stop that almost didn't happen* – found me in a conversation with the wife of my then-husband's friend. She equipped me with a bag of used skincare, and I was so ready – so open to change – my only questions were around what it would take to make it to the top of this company.

If you looked into the snow globe of my life leading up to that pivotal moment, you'd see a professional mom with the perfect marriage, the perfect home, the perfect children and all the glamour of a high-producing pharma sales rep.

A company car and reward trips, especially back in the 90s, meant you'd "arrived" in my industry. Along with expense accounts to wine and dine physicians, made it difficult for anyone to see why I'd want something different.

What you didn't see was the empty vessel that I had become. *None of this felt comfortable, yet I was functioning in the most "comfortable" life.*

Do you know anyone living for the weekend – but when the weekend comes, it's a food shop + clean the house + run kids to activities and birthday parties and close it all out with Sunday night stomachache? I did. And it was me.

The Story Behind the Glory

Within five months, I soared to the top of the skincare company. Five months.

What never made the spotlight was the fact that with 15+ years in pharma sales and just as many years spent on personal growth, coaching certifications, late nights and early mornings of master coach training – I was no overnight success.

I started to feel after a few years at my former company that there was something different out there for me. I was confident I was meant for more – and it took me two years to do anything about it. In spite of the accolades, the relationships and of course, an amazing paycheck I had built for myself, I had to make a move.

Now a single mom with three young kids relying on me, I took a leap of faith – armed once again with not much more than my grit, work ethic and years of personal development – and started what is now a global team at my forever home.

Soon after, in 2013, I published my first book, titled The Art of Getting What You Want: How to Cultivate the Happiness, Health and Wealth You Desire, inspiring solo-preneurs all over the world to reach for their dreams. To me, **network marketing is not just business – it's big business** – and the lessons learned along the way apply to all entrepreneurs.

The stories we tell ourselves around what's hard, what's not working, why we should start Monday are just that – stories.

My passion for helping others to develop self-love, self-reliance, and an abundance mindset continue to fuel what I do daily. There's no such thing as "arriving," especially in this amazing industry! So many lessons learned along the way, but one of the most important lies in the word *expansion*.

Expansion comes with adversity – and what needs to happen to get to the other side. Have you ever really thought about how hard it is to constrict, expand, and then go back? Acknowledge yourself for all you've been through and find the gratitude in it all.

Watering the Grass…

The best way to describe how I felt when I was looking to make a shift? Ready for expansion.

I'll never forget being told, "the grass is never greener on the other side" when I made my move to my second company. Turns out for me it was – and continues to be.

By taking action and staying in the promise to myself – I created an even greater income than my previous company for myself and my family in just 23 months.

It was never my focus, but in the process of staying clear on my goals, I have won almost every award, and I continue to strive to be my best self.

After making a bold move and trusting my intuition, I find myself as a top international speaker at the helm of a global team, but most of all, I am proud that I have taken a whole team to new heights. *This is what keeps me engaged after nine years – nine years!*

Many of my leaders have earned amazing incomes and continue to build their life by design. I coach and train, leading from a place of service, and this has allowed thousands of people some incredible outcomes – for some, this is a little extra income a month; for some, it is a life-changing yearly income.

There's a saying I love in this industry, and it goes like this: *we all put our pants on the same way each morning – one leg at a time.*

What happens when we're dressed for the day, the promise to ourselves we live in, determines much of the rest.

Get out there and make decisions that make you proud.

Here are my *3 Tell-All's* for you:

1. Do your homework and make sure that you have a good understanding of the industry and all that's possible.
2. Always ask for referrals.
3. Reach down deep into your organization, don't rely on others to identify the gems on your team. Make sure your team knows who you are, and you know who they are.

If you could go back in time when you started your first business in network marketing and you could start all over again, what would you do differently?

I would embrace this philosophy sooner: Some will. Some won't. So what? Who's next?

———————

Lisa DeMayo is a coach, trainer, public speaker, top-level network marketer and entrepreneur who calls New Jersey her home. For over 20 years, she has trained in the modalities of Somatic Work, Ontological Coaching, Neurolinguistic Programming, Reiki, Hypno-Therapy, and more and is now a life, leadership and executive coach.

Lisa DeMayo is the Co-founder and CEO of LiVenUp! She has 15 years of experience in the pharmaceutical industry and is a successful entrepreneur. Lisa is masterful at team building and has grown two international distributorships in the health and wellness industry with over 200,000 members. Her passion for helping others has prompted her to become a serial entrepreneur in the health and wellness industry.

Lisa is a published author. Her first book, The Art of Getting What You Want: How to Cultivate the Happiness, Health and Wealth You Desire, includes a foreword by Jack Canfield of Chicken Soup for the Soul.

Lisa has been on the cover of Empowering Women Magazine, Star Magazine, and Industry Magazine. Her story has been featured in Prosper Magazine, The Flip Flop CEO, Networking Times, 25A Magazine and many trade publications. She can be heard on podcasts all over the globe talking about health and wellness and the mind, body, spirit connection.

In addition to Life Coach, International Public Speaker and Network Marketer, she is also mom to 3 beautiful children: Gianna, Victoria, and Nick.

Excited for the upcoming chapters of her own life, Lisa is looking forward to more time with her newly blended family.

18

ANGELA MARTINI

"You were born to scale heights higher than you have still imagined and uniquely created to fulfill the whispers of our soul; all you need to DO is LISTEN…"

Steep mountains, long cold winters, rich history and tradition, forged my humble upbringing in the Austrian Alps. I was raised with strong family values and a strict upbringing as the oldest of three girls.

And so, I grew up in a small town surrounded by farms and animals with ironclad rules, stereotypical gender roles and a deep burning for freedom inside me. I reflect back on my childhood with fond memories and a deep sense of belonging but also confusion as I had so many limits imposed on me by my circumstances.

I have always been strong-willed, positive, happy and unafraid to try new things, much to my mother and grandmother's dismay.

My happiest memories are on the back of my pony Jenny; I would ride with my long brown hair waving in the wind and dreaming of a life far away from home. Somehow, I knew that I would have to leave my homeland to grow and expand and make my mark.

At the age of fifteen, I fell in love for the first time. He was eighteen, tall, handsome and had been raised in Canada. After a three-year romance and long-distance relationship, I decided to leave it all behind, my country, my family, and my beloved sisters and followed the call to freedom and the land of opportunity. I immigrated to Canada at the tender age of eighteen.

Today, I realize that I don't allow myself very often to look back at the moment that changed the course of life. I left my parents and crying sisters at the airport in Munich in 1983. I looked back at my mother's teary eyes, and it would be years until I returned back home.

I arrived in a foreign country with limited English language skills, all my belongings stuffed into two suitcases and many challenges I never imagined. Many nights I would cry myself to sleep, suffering from unbearable homesickness and the confusion of loving it all the while.

In the next few decades, I embarked on years of growth, hard work, night school, a University education as a dental hygienist, divorce, financial hardship and multiple jobs to make ends meet. One of the most positive anchors in my life was becoming a fitness instructor. I enjoyed creating an impact as a fitness leader and the thousands of classes and students that would follow me for years. Somehow, I knew that there was more for me, and I was driven by that sense of impacting people's lives in a much bigger way.

Looking back now, these challenges prepared me to be open to finding the love of my life and the family and freedom I desired. My second husband, Joe, brought new energy into my life and his upbringing and our values aligned as he is the son of immigrant parents. He dreamt big dreams just like me and encouraged me to continue to grow, expand and always be in the YES energy, and that made me open...

In my late forties, after years of running small businesses and twin motherhood, I found myself having gained unwanted pounds and was introduced to a product line that became a lifeline. A new horizon appeared, and I was introduced to network marketing. I was very skeptical at first, but the product supported a result that was undeniable.

At the age of 47, I stepped onto the fitness stage, a lifelong goal, in the best shape of my life with my family cheering me on.

The manifestation of this dream and the persistence of my enrolling sponsor made me take a deeper look and attend a few events. Events are where decisions are made, and hope is inspired, and so I began to listen, learn and immerse myself in the training and actions of those that had the results I desired. There something very powerful in the energy of ignorance on fire, and within a few short months, I reached the top rank of the company.

In this business model, I started to eliminate the fear of success, the fear of not being good enough, and the fear of wanting more. When I chose to step into leadership, I knew that I had to level up, I knew I had to lead, I knew there was no more hiding. I became a student of the network marketing profession, and started to work on me. I found strength in helping people get better physically and supporting them on their journey.

The more I lost myself in the service of others and invested in helping people reach their goals, I forgot all about the things that might hold me back. I started to believe like never before, and magic started to happen. Thousands of people have shown up, and it has created a ripple effect that continues today.

The most powerful example of breaking through myself imposed limitations was setting a goal of reaching my ideal yearly income. I remember the day I decided that it was possible for me and that I saw myself achieving this milestone. All of my life experiences have served me well in being compassionate and resilient, and my heart grew fonder of helping more and more people.

This profession has continued to bless me with rich relationships, travel, incredible experiences and opportunities like being part of this book. I have become a bestselling author, an international speaker and advocate for the network marketing profession. Not all your days in this industry will be rosy and there will be ups and downs, but you will never run out of opportunity to grow, and this is priceless, especially for a girl from a small town in Austria.

Today, I find myself in the right place, aligned with my purpose and honoured to share this part of my journey. I am in gratitude for all the hardships that have allowed me to find my light. When we realize that everything in life happens for us, we can clearly see the gift in the struggle and resulting personal growth.

There are many more unwritten chapters and experiences right around the corner. Be open to the possibilities that this profession offers as a training ground for personal excellence and servant leadership.

Here are my 3 "TELL ALL" tips I want to share with you:

1. *LEARN TO SAY YES*

There is great power in being in the YES energy. The most important YES is to say YES to YOU first. YES to you deserving all the success you can imagine and YES to all-important self-care and the time required to cultivate a mindset that allows you to be – do and have all you desire.

You are your most valuable asset and will need to enlist the support of your team. Say YES to accepting help and teamwork. Trust that you have the power within you to build the life and freedom you desire. Say YES to giving it the time required for you to continue to step into your higher self. Say YES to leading in your own unique way and continue to grow as you go! This is a marathon, not a sprint.

YES, you got this!

2. *LEARN TO SAY NO*

Knowing when and what to say NO to is an art and takes practice. You might have heard this, *"the yes's built my business, and the no's built my character."* NO can be a powerful instrument of integrity and setting clear boundaries. It often takes courage to say NO, and it can hard to receive but setting limits early on in the business will allow for more balance during your build.

Saying NO to the things that are not serving your top priorities and learning to say NO to unrealistic expectations eventually will lead to you being able to say YES more often later.

3. *YOUR STORY WILL EVOLVE*

As your business grows, so will you... and even when the ups and downs of business will have you experience the highest highs and some inevitable lows, it will all be worth it.

What matters most is that you continue to grow and that you always keep your Highs –> Low and your Lows –> High. Find a pace that is sustainable and anchor yourself in belief and protect it.

Keep your inner circle small and create a support network of people outside of your success line to keep you balanced. Continue to see the beauty of this profession in the eyes of a "newbie" this will keep your feet on the ground.

Dare to Dream and put in the work to Win.

I believe in YOU!

Angela

If you could go back in time and you were just starting your first business in direct sales and you could start all never again, what would you do differently?

I would trust myself more, value my journey and growth and my own unique experience in this extraordinary profession that is network marketing. I consider myself very fortunate that it chose me.

…And by the way, it will always be a business of doing the basics better and consistently.

STEP 1: Know your WHY and driver (it will change over time)

STEP 2: Decide on your goal – make it specific

STEP 3: Create a solid plan and get accountable

STEP 5: Act on that plan, act on that plan, and act on that plan ...until

STEP 6: Review your action and results, re-evaluate and course correct for success

STEP 7: **REPEAT**

Angela was born in the rugged Austrian Alps and at an early age was introduced to the value of hard work and resilience.

In her late teens she immigrated to Canada with just two suitcases and big dreams, many of them already realized.

She is the mother of identical twin daughters and has been married for over 25 years to the love of her life, Joe.

Angela is a passionate entrepreneur with a diverse background in health and wellness, spanning almost four decades.

In her late forties, Angela was introduced to a network marketing distributed product line, which allowed her to step onto the fitness stage in the best shape of her life.

She fell in love with the culture, leadership of her partner company and the profession of network marketing and went on to build a team of thousands. Today, Angela continues to be a successful network marketing leader and advocate for the network marketing profession. This growth inspired platform has propelled her to become a best-selling author and international speaker.

Angela's mission is to inspire others to create a life of freedom and choice. She accomplishes this by inviting synergistic partnerships, providing mentorship to those that choose to co-create with a common goal and unlock their full potential.

19

ELAINE WHITE

"The mind is everything. What you think about you become."

~ Buddha

Has it happened to you yet? Have you had the most popular fantasy in network marketing? It's a dream about a total stranger calling you, expressing interest in your products, asking probing questions about the income opportunity, and within days joins your team and quickly becomes your biggest distributor.

As fate would have it, in April of 2007, I was that total stranger and someone's dream come true. While getting a manicure, I glanced up and saw remarkable before and after pictures and called the rep. The rest is history. That phone call was life-changing for me, for her and for thousands of others. That is how my journey began.

My husband and I had recently returned from China with our baby girl and I wanted nothing more than to stay home with her. I happily walked away from a very successful, twenty-five-year career in corporate America as VP of Human Resources to start our family.

The challenge was we had was a lifestyle that required both of our incomes. I'm sure you can imagine my quandary. Like many new moms, I wanted to figure out how to be a full-time, stay-at-home mom and contribute financially to my family.

When I learned about residual income, I thought, "OMG – THIS IS IT, I would be negligent to not do it – we CAN have it all." I immediately realized I had found the answer I had been praying for, a way to work from home, around my family's schedule, by simply sharing products I believed it. I was ALL IN and was determined to succeed because this opportunity would allow me to fulfill my true calling, being a mom to our daughter.

I kicked off my business off with immense pride *"I've found my second career, join me!"* I would tell anyone and everyone. I had many people jump in with me as I had a large professional network, and people trusted my business sense, so I was off and running in no time. I have since learned that when someone has rapid success in this industry, it's often due to their insatiable desire to succeed; I had that desire in spades.

As with any new business, there are growing pains and challenges, and with mine, it was me. I was the challenge and the problem I had to fix. I acted like a manager, actually a supervisor, and not a leader. I had forgotten to take off my corporate hat and played the role of a boss to my team, which didn't bode well. My behavior lost me a dear friend that I still miss today. When I realized the error of my ways, I devoured every CD, book and training I could find on leadership, team dynamics and this industry. I quickly learned how to lead, motivate and inspire people, and THAT is when the fun and explosion began.

Over the course of the next 13 years, I have been blessed to reach top leadership levels in two companies and earned multiple incentives and perks. I have met people that I now consider family and have more love for people around the world than I ever thought humanly possible. The lifestyle income has had its perks, and my family is forever grateful but "doing life" with my peers is the icing on the cake and brings priceless joy.

In 2020 I turned 64. Andy, my husband of over 30 years, is 69, and our daughter Elizabeth is 19. She is currently a freshman at Arizona State University (go Sun Devils). Thanks to this industry, we have been able to live where we want, travel when and where we want, live life on our timing and without an alarm clock, and we give thanks every single day for those blessings.

If you are new to this industry or are considering it, I can't impress upon you enough the altruistic benefits that come with it. People lifting up each other, working toward comment goals and dreams, all while becoming lifelong friends. My favorite thing about this industry is that it is the polar opposite of the typical business environment of dog eat dog. It's exactly like Zig Zigler said: "Help enough people get what they want, and you'll get everything you want."

Another thing I love about this industry is school is never out – we are constantly learning and growing from each other. I look forward to sharing a few tips with you that really shifted my career in the hopes that you will experience the same effect in yours. I also hope that should we have the occasion to meet at some point in the future that you will share your story and tips. We are all better together, and even though I may not know you, this chapter is me sharing my personal story and lessons, so I feel like we are already friends.

Tip #1 – It's Not About You

If you are asked to do ANYTHING – a training, a call, host an event, be on a panel, present at a meeting, anything – DO IT, even if you don't think you are ready and don't feel like you'll do a good job – DO IT ANYWAY! A side benefit is you will grow by pushing your limits, but most importantly, do it for the field. You do it so they can see you and know they can do it too. When you have the opportunity to be on stage, remember you aren't up there for you and your glory, you are up there as an example to others of what's possible. You are a hope and dream builder up there. When you live in that mindset, you will be asked again and again to show up and will become the true leader you are.

A call from the President of the company came hours after I was promoted to a top rank; she asked me to do a 45-minute training to the entire company in 3 days on any topic of my choice. I was petrified, but I did it anyway. I joined a new company in 2012 and in my first month was invited to train on a corporate-wide call; I was new and green and felt totally unprepared, but I did it anyway. I was asked to be a co-host for an event with over 10,000 people, and I felt overweight and overwhelmed, thought I'd surely wet myself on stage, but I did it anyway. Several times I was asked to be on a panel at our national conference, I was incredibly intimated by the genius of other panelists, but each time I did it anyway. Today I am asked on a regular basis to train and lead events for my company; why? Because I did it when I wasn't ready…. I pushed myself to show others they could do it, and as a result, not only did I continue to grow, but dozens and dozens of leaders I mentored became some of the most gifted trainers and highly respected speakers in the industry. Any part I played in their success feels better than anything money can buy. In summary, showing up, doing the scary or glamourous task, isn't for or about you; always do it and do it for others.

Tip #2 – Recognition

My love language is gifting, so this came naturally to me. But recognition, especially in our industry, is more than gifts. It's a call out on social media; it's a handwritten note, it's a certificate printed on a home printer. It can be a Tiffany & Co. gift or a piece of paper; I found the size or price doesn't matter. What matters is the sincerity of what you are recognizing and the consistency in giving praise. We often hear it said, "Men die for it, and babies cry for it"- why? Because it makes everyone feel good. I suggest, even if you have a team of one, you have a monthly recognition program to call out the wins, however small, that can be celebrated.

My warning is this – do not let it be a time or money suck. I made that mistake in my first two years. I spent WAY too much, gave gifts that my downline couldn't duplicate, and spent hours on it rather than on income-producing activity. Recognition is key to the overall success of a team, but it must be simple, consistent and easily duplicatable so as your leaders grow, they can keep it going. The bottom line is to think it through before you start, have a written plan and a budget and stick to it.

Tip #3 – TRACK IT – 3 Success Factors

I have a love affair with excel, so that's how I personally track everything, but you can use whatever is most convenient for you;

pen and paper work great! The point is as the CEO of your business, you need to treat it like a business, and that requires knowing real time where things stand financially. On a daily basis, I track my personal and team volume, my new starts, any trip points, and some of my key leader's numbers as well. Doing this allows me to compare month over month (on each day) to see how the month is progressing to the prior month(s). It's far better to know before the end of the month that you are going to come up short or get super close to a new goal, so you have time to do something about it.

Along with having a massive desire, I sincerely believe that focusing on and tracking the following three success factors on a daily basis is key to success. The three success factors are Personal Development, Activity and Plugging In. I developed a simple tracker to keep me honest and visually on track. I suggest you make one that you can visually see if all are being done on a consistent basis. Doing all three of these simple things equally will result in success – do it and just watch it happen!

In closing this chapter, I would say give yourself grace, never ever compare your progress to others and appreciate that this is YOUR JOURNEY. Dreams do come true in this industry if you work for them, so consider using the weekly success tracker to keep you on your path.

If you could go back in time when you started your first business in network marketing and you could start all over again, what would you do differently?

Easy answer- dream bigger sooner. I started with what I thought was a big vision, a big dream – but now I know it was not. In Corporate America, I was used to ceilings and limits, so I didn't grasp the concept of having a bodacious dream. I set my sights on levels I had previously achieved and felt comfortable there. I now know that ANYTHING is possible if your mind sees and believes it. An unwavering vision of your huge dream will drive you to do things, it will attract things, and it will propel you. I wish I knew that sooner, not only for my sake but all the team dream building conversations I had early on would have been far more reaching to help them uncover their deepest and BIGGEST desires.

Mom, Wife, CEO, International Trainer and Speaker. Elaine enjoyed a 25-year business career leading global Human Resources organizations; she was also part of the Mergers and Acquisitions Executive Team, leading due diligence on more than a dozen corporate acquisitions. In 2007 Elaine joined Network Marketing, and her lifelong passion for helping others realize their full potential was a perfect fit, and she quickly soared by helping others. Seeing the best in people and situations, coupled with her deep-rooted happiness and joy for living, is what Elaine is known best for.

20

WAYMATEA ELLIS

On a December evening in the late '70s, my love to lead was born. I was four years old. On that particular night, I sat in a crowded gym, with long white stockings and black polished Mary Janes. My legs swung back and forth under my red Christmas dress with the white lace trim. I looked up at my father. The high school band had just finished a holiday song, and he was their conductor. My eyes went from him to the students playing, to the response of the crowd. I was so proud to watch him conducting, fascinated by his "magic wand" and the way he could use his arms and facial expressions, his eyes and body, to bring together such a joyful noise! The applause swelled in the echoing room—a loud, unmistakable sound of approval. My breath caught—was this the moment? My father looked over at me, smiled, and nodded. I stood up, my steps clicking on the gym floor to where he stood.

I could feel the audience get quiet. It seemed awfully quiet—I could hear someone adjust their chair, someone talking… small sounds that seemed so amplified. My father placed a large wooden box in front of his conductor's music stand. I held out my hand to be helped up onto the box. He smiled and handed me his conductor's baton, and as I adjusted my stance, I glanced up to look at the band members. Each was holding their orchestral instrument, and the one I locked eyes with smiled warmly with me. I lifted the baton, and both arms ready, I counted them in: One, and two, and three, and four, and... music filled the air. And as I counted and moved my arms the way we had practiced, an impressionable young girl got her first taste of a powerful magic – the sound of leadership.

By 2014, I was a married, homeschooling, professional musician, and former teacher. I loved our family's lifestyle of performing, touring, and exceeding in one of my favourite passions: music. Homeschooling was a dream come true made possible by the support of my husband, and I was really enjoying being a stay-at-home mom. My spouse and I worked hard on our reggae music project with our friends, touring the country and even scoring a JUNO nomination. But difficult things came to pass, and the marriage was not to last. We began the painful process of separation. Despite the tangles involved in the dismantling, I wanted to preserve stability for our children. I wanted to keep the beautiful closeness that we had created as a traditional homeschooling family. It has always meant so much to me to be the primary adult in my children's daytime hours. However, after my spouse moved out, I found myself in unbearably lean times that stretched me financially, mentally, and physically in ways that I will never forget.

On August 11th, 2015, inspired by an Abraham-Hicks recording, I took pen to paper. You know how you write those, "I'm so happy and grateful now that..." letters? Well, I wrote things like *"I'm so happy and grateful now that I am stable as a homeschooling mom, now that the girls are happy, and our lives are abundant, and we live in a safe and warm home, and we have a LOT of food in the pantry, and we go travelling, and we laugh a lot…"* I wrote all this and much more—literally 22 pages of gratitude for my not yet realized dreams. From that day forward, I read it every single day, once in the morning and once at night. I even included, *"I look and feel younger than ever before! It's like I reversed the ageing process—my face is smooth, glowing—it looks so young!"* Spoiler: the Universe was listening. More on that in a moment.

In the fall of 2015, I was unable to keep up with my mortgage and the repairs of the home I had worked so hard to purchase. I packed up my children and our belongings and walked away. I said goodbye to the deck my father had built for us and the two beautiful cherry trees my children loved to climb. I felt devastated. As a rather public person and performer, I felt visible and vulnerable, embarrassed and alone. And while our band essentially fell apart, I took on everything else I knew how to do—massage therapy, substitute teaching, respite care for children, artist in residence, and I have to tell you: there are only 24 hours in a day. There were nights when I would wake up in a sweating panic; in the short sleep I was allowing myself. Most nights, I would get just four hours of sleep. I was burning out, and I was scared. I sometimes wondered if I would die in my sleep, from the crippling anxiety or panic attacks, or from sheer exhaustion. At the end of every month, there was less money, bigger bills, and it got worse as the months continued. And the most heartbreaking part was that my children very much did NOT have a happy, present mother. They had an exhausted, preoccupied parent, who snapped easily at them, and barely looked up from her work long enough to participate in the ideal family dynamic she was striving for.

The night I remember vividly was very cold, close to Christmas of

2015. It was the dead of winter, and the furnace in our home was not working properly. I was out of money and opening envelopes warning for disconnection of utilities when a friend came to check up on me. She saw the nearly empty fridge and pantry, and she noticed the cold inside the house. She helped me to get the furnace going and then urged me to ask for help, at least just to get me through the season. I suppose both pride and brain exhaustion had blinded me up until this moment, to truly see how deeply I had spiralled. But through her eyes, I could see that I was slipping into a very bad place, both financially and mentally. Reluctantly, I found myself at the local food bank, and because it was so close to Christmas, we received an additional home delivery from Santa's Anonymous. I still remember sending my children upstairs to shield them from knowing how their gifts would get under the tree, and as local firemen climbed the steps to our home, carrying the bags of donation, I felt a wave of shame in my heart. But something told me to stay completely and utterly present to the moment. To receive with grace. I looked in their eyes, received the gifts, and I said sincerely, "Thank You." And in that profound, life-changing moment, I decided that I had gone *far enough* down this spiral, and I was done with it. It was my Day of Disgust.

By April 2016, we had already moved homes twice. Despite little evidence that it was working, I continued to read my 22-page letter and practiced meditations and gratitude, morning and night.

A friend came over for a massage, and just as we were getting started, she said, face down in the cradle, "Way, I have something to run by you." At that moment, I became covered in goosebumps from the back of my neck, all the way down my body. I hesitated, literally looked up at the ceiling, and I thought, "Is this it?" She continued, "I met a lady, and she's looking for distributors for a skincare line.

It's super holistic. You know, I don't know much about it, but if you want to go check out the presentation, apparently you can make a lot of money." I was like, "Uh-Huh!" Because A: I LOVE skincare, and B: "Yes Please!" to making some money!

Here's a bit of background. I had been a network marketer before. Twenty years earlier, while attending university, I saw an amazing opportunity with a well-established company and went all-in with a good friend of mine. We showed the presentation on campus, in my apartment, and anywhere else we could meet up with prospects, but we never successfully recruited anyone. Each month's cost was outside our student budget, so we were a bit stretched, but we saw the vision and truly believed that we could be featured in the shiny magazine with the other millionaires one day. We eventually went to the annual conference held in our home city of Edmonton to fully participate and get pumped up for our inevitable success! And that's when we realized we were in the wrong company. The more people we met, it became very obvious that we simply didn't fit in at all—we felt very uncomfortable and out of place. We left early and eventually quit altogether. Looking back, I can see that although the culture of that company was out of moral alignment with our views, the experience planted a seed for me that I would, one day, harness the power of the network marketing industry. With the right people, the right product, and the right culture, I envisioned myself soaring in this field. I flirted with a few other companies over the years but had not yet felt that moment when I could 'ring the bell' for having found a perfect fit. Until now.

I went to the presentation and learned the details. I fell in love with the story behind the product right away, but I was a bit skeptical about the results. I asked the host dozens of questions at the end of the presentation. I listened to her answers. The business sounded amazing, but I didn't want to be too spontaneous and make a mistake. So that night, I lay awake with a sample of the cream on my face and asked for a sign that I should NOT do this. I waited for some kind of boil, a horrible rash, or something to happen for me to say NO. I woke up in the morning (rash free!) but having hardly slept at all because I could NOT stop the feeling that something BIG was happening here. So I did it. I enrolled with my May 1st rent. The date was April 17th, 2016. Exactly eight months and six days after I wrote my 22-page letter to the Universe.

I am happy to tell you that not only did I pay my rent on time on May 1st, but there have been so many more benefits from that decision to say YES. My skin looks younger than when I started. My stress levels are down, and my sleep cycles are healthy. I'm playing music again, among other joyful projects. Life feels spacious, full of dreams and choices. I have the most amazing mentors in the world, and the best-extended family I could hope for. Network marketing has offered me restoration of my personal power. My steam fuels my dream! What a difference from feeling trapped and afraid. I feel excited and totally blessed as the side-gig world has emerged, and I'm ready for it.

And for my daughters? They have a healthy mom, a LAUGHING mom, a peaceful home, and stability. They have the confidence to take action on their dreams, and that is an amazing gift. It makes me so proud to be their living example of turning adversity into a powerful success.

It hasn't been all easy. I have faced some personal challenges while building my organization. One has been my fear of failure. In the past, when I would experience failure in my network marketing business, it shut me down. I didn't ever want to get things wrong! Even though I tell my children that it's OK to make mistakes, I was much harder on myself. I have learned that the greatest leaders embrace failure, and in fact, fail forward.

Another challenge I faced was the fear of stepping on people's toes. I would hesitate to share my thoughts or questions around people I looked up to. Even though in my music career, I didn't shy away from being the 'front woman', and as a teacher, of course, I was often at the front of the class giving instruction, I have only recently come into a more comfortable place to 'shine' in my organization.

Thirdly, I have worked diligently to reframe my brain and beliefs around dollars and abundance. I love that we can retrain our habitual thought patterns, and I have done so intentionally. Making peace with and trusting money may be the most significant advancement I have made. I will continue to work on this piece, and I embrace that personal development is never finished.

My Three Tell All Tips

1. I believe the secret to success in leadership in network marketing is to work from the heart. The first time I experienced this was looking into that band that night, at four years old. I saw the faces of sweet kindness and encouragement. I trained my eyes upon the best, most uplifting people. And what I have developed since then is the ability to give freely of my heart even when people aren't ready to elevate to that. Refrain from gossip; rather, see and speak from your heart, and you will bring out the best in others.

2. Step into the spaces that people create for you. Remember the wooden step my father put in place for me to be able to reach

the music stand and to be seen by the band? When someone offers you help, take it. Coaching? Yes, please. Mentorship? It's essential to your growth. If you aren't stepping into the spaces where you are the greenest, know the least, or have something to learn from those in your circle, you are playing too small. And if you aren't receiving the help being offered to you, your ego may be preventing you from realizing your dreams.

3. Practice the Magic. The baton my father passed to me felt like a wand, and I couldn't wait to use it. I invite you to explore your creative power, to compose the harmonious and beautiful song that is your life. Write your 22-page letter, a diary entry from yourself five years from now, create a dream board, go on rampages of appreciation. Harness the magic the Universe offers you with the law of attraction by being selective in your associations, your thoughts, and the words you speak. You are capable of exceeding the heights of your grandest dreams. Seize those tools and RUN HARD. You've got this.

You know if I was to go back to the beginning, if I could whisper the secret of success to myself when I was just starting out, I would say – it is NOT about the product. It is about personal development. Read every book, listen to every recording, and devour every training available to you, so that you grow your belief in yourself, your leadership, and the profession of network marketing. Deep inside you, there is a divine gift. Personal development will not only help you to unwrap this gift, but it will compel you to share this gift with everyone you meet. Then I would give myself a hug and say, – you have made an amazing decision. I'm so proud of you. Now buckle up for the adventure of a lifetime!

Waymatea Ellis is a network marketing leader, mentor, motivational speaker, minister and musician. She offers a unique approach to success, wellness, and living life authentically, peacefully and joyfully. Among many accolades for her teaching and music career, Waymatea has been awarded Global TV's Woman of Vision, University of Alberta's Alumni Award of Excellence, and a JUNO nomination for "Reggae Recording of the Year." Way is a homeschooling mom of two girls and makes her home in Edmonton, AB, Canada.

Final Words

THANK YOU!

We are grateful and feel honoured that you took the time to read our book. To learn more about the authors or connect with them, please visit our Speaker's page:

www.abeautifullifemagazine.com/20-powerful-women

Lastly, we would like to invite you to join us every week on **The TRUE THAT Show**! A show about Lifepreneurship presented with wit, humour, and banter by Deborah Drummond and Caroline Blanchard.

Lifepreneurship is about developing an authentic, personal vision for life and then going for it. It's about awakening to the opportunities around us and setting audacious goals. It's about taking action and making a difference. It's about taking time out for reflection so we can renew ourselves for the road ahead.

In The TRUE THAT Show, you will hear real talks with real people from different walks of life who all have one thing in common: their uniqueness.

Join Deborah and Caroline, who have done thousands of presentations together and are appreciated for their wit, humour, emotional intelligence, life experiences, and saying things how they really are, on their journey of discovery, growth, awareness, and personal development.

This weekly show about real subjects, real people, and real-life will leave you wanting to be the best version of yourself.

Audio version: www.ctrnetwork.com/truethat
Video Version: https://tinyurl.com/y2es6rxn

Other Publications

Other Publications from TRUE THAT Media coming in 2021

20 Influential Men in Network Marketing Tell All

20 Outstanding Couples in Network Marketing Tell All

Made in the USA
Monee, IL
09 February 2021